JESUIT AND
ZEN MASTER

JESUIT AND ZEN MASTER

A Life of Hugo M. Enomiya-Lassalle

URSULA BAATZ

Translated by Dennis Johnson

ORBIS BOOKS
Maryknoll, New York 10545

Founded in 1970, Orbis Books endeavors to publish works that enlighten the mind, nourish the spirit, and challenge the conscience. The publishing arm of the Maryknoll Fathers and Brothers, Orbis seeks to explore the global dimensions of the Christian faith and mission, to invite dialogue with diverse cultures and religious traditions, and to serve the cause of reconciliation and peace. The books published reflect the views of their authors and do not represent the official position of the Maryknoll Society. To learn more about Maryknoll and Orbis Books, please visit our website at www.orbisbooks.com.

English translation copyright © 2026 by Orbis Books

First German edition: Ursula Baatz, *H. M. Enomiya-Lasalle: Jesuit und Zen-Lehrer ; Brückenbauer zwischen Ost und West*, Herder Verlag 2004; reprint by Topos: Hugo Enomiya-Lassale, Mittler zwischen Buddismus und Christentum.

Published by Orbis Books, Box 302, Maryknoll, NY 10545-0302.

Manufactured in the United States of America

Library of Congress Cataloging-in-Publication Data

Names: Baatz, Ursula author | Johnson, Dennis, 1981- translator
Title: Jesuit and zen master : a life of Hugo M. Enomiya Lassalle / Ursula Baatz ; translated by Dennis Johnson.
Other titles: Hugo Makibi Enomiya-Lassalle. English
Description: Maryknoll, NY : Orbis Books, [2026] | "First German edition: Ursula Baatz, *H. M. Enomiya-Lasalle: Jesuit und Zen-Lehrer ; Brückenbauer zwischen Ost und West*, Herder Verlag 2004" | Includes bibliographical references.
Identifiers: LCCN 2025036726 (print) | LCCN 2025036727 (ebook) | ISBN 9781626986466 paperback | ISBN 9798888661000 epub
Subjects: LCSH: Enomiya-Lassalle, Hugo M. (Hugo Makibi), 1898-1990 | Jesuits—Biography | Missionaries—Japan—Biography | Missionaries—Germany—Biography | LCGFT: Biographies
Classification: LCC BV3457.E56 B22413 2026 (print) | LCC BV3457.E56 (ebook)
LC record available at https://lccn.loc.gov/2025036726
LC ebook record available at https://lccn.loc.gov/2025036727

Contents

Foreword

Jerry Brown

I first met Father Lassalle, SJ, in the summer of 1986. I had traveled to China and stopped briefly in Tokyo. While there, I decided to see if I could find a Jesuit who knew something about Zen meditation, a subject I first became interested in many years before when I was governor of California (1975–1983). I first learned about meditation as a Jesuit novice and years later made many visits to the San Francisco Zen Center. Nevertheless I never took the time to actually practice zazen, the unique form of sitting meditation that forms the heart of Zen Buddhism. So when I arrived in Tokyo, I went directly to Sophia University and asked if there was any Jesuit there who could tell me about the practice of Zen in Japan. The woman at the reception desk made a call and then told me that Father Dumoulin would speak with me.

Soon the Jesuit priest and I were engaged in a long discussion of Zen Buddhism and its history in Japan. Father Dumoulin wrote a definitive history of Buddhism and was deeply knowledgeable. After an hour or so, he said that he was merely a scholar and if I wanted to understand the practice of Zen, I should meet Father Enomiya-Lassalle. Which I did. And for the next several hours, I sat rapt in attention as Father Lassalle patiently laid out his view of the current state of religion and the new consciousness that was emerging in the world.

He said the ancient Greeks did not think logically until the time of Plato.This represented a radical shift similar to the one going on now. He said people know only what they experience and that theology as we have known it is finished. For a priest trained in the conservative tradition of pre–Vatican II Catholicism, that was quite a statement. I asked him how he could still be a Catholic, and he said he "never left the Church. There is nothing better. I love the Church but it will change." He also mentioned that Heidegger said philosophy is over. This was a heavy message, but Father Lassalle's manner and presence was so authentic and so caring that I pressed him to know how I could learn more about what he was talking about. He said Koun Yamada Roshi was one of the best Zen teachers in Japan and I should meet him.

So the next day, I visited Yamada at the hospital in Tokyo where he was the chief administrator. Yamada was not a Buddhist priest but a respected lay teacher who had a zendo in Kamakura where both Japanese and foreign students came to practice Zen meditation. He invited me to come there and learn for myself.

I went back to California and within a few weeks came back to Japan and found a place to live in Kamakura and started doing zazen for two hours each evening. I stayed for six months, during which I made a number of weeklong retreats called sesshins—full days devoted to sitting on a cushion, face to the wall, meditating in complete silence. Two of these retreats took place in the mountains west of Tokyo at Shinmeikutsu. This was the Zen center that Lassalle was able to construct after a protracted struggle in raising the money and getting the final approval of his Jesuit superiors.

Enomiya-Lassalle was no ordinary man. He fought in World War I and was wounded on the Western Front. During World War II, he was in Hiroshima the day the atomic bomb dropped but survived and was able to make his way out of the city.

Schooled in the horrors of these terrible wars, he nonetheless maintained a positive and utterly engaging attitude.

Shinmeikutsu was exactly what you would imagine a Zen mountain retreat would look like—wooden buildings with simple accommodations, a hall for meals, and a large meditation room with tatami mats on raised platforms. In the middle was a large rock with a cross on it that served as the altar where Father Lassalle celebrated Mass each morning. The routine of the sesshin was silence, a bit of physical labor, and ten hours of meditation spread throughout the day and evening. Unlike the traditional Jesuit meditation, there was no object to meditate on such as a virtue or a scene from the life of Christ. In zazen, you partially close your eyes and just follow your breathing with full attention. Thoughts drift by but you do your best to let them go.

The zendo in Shinmeikutsu, with a tatami mat on the platform. In the middle of the room is a huge rock with a small cross lying flat on top of the stones.

After a few days of this, your mind is more quiet and in a receptive state. Each morning Father Lassalle would get up from his tatami mat and approach the altar and begin saying the Mass. When he got to the place where it was time to consecrate the host, he slowly uttered the words, "This is my body." At that moment, I strongly felt that "my body" included the host, Father Lassalle, and everyone in the hall.

Enomiya-Lassalle has been gone for more than thirty years but the story of his life remains vitally relevant in this time of hard-edged beliefs that increasingly divide societies into warring camps. Lassalle was brought up in strict Catholicism and Jesuit obedience. Yet, his open spirit and direct experience of human violence at its worst led him to transcend his parochial upbringing and rigid Jesuit training. A lesson for our time. When he started practicing zazen, his church taught that it was sinful to participate in the rituals of another religion. Undaunted, and without giving up his faith or his Jesuit vows, Lassalle found a way to introduce a central Buddhist form of contemplation and get it adopted in many parts of the world. He outlasted determined Jesuit and ecclesiastical opposition and inspired thousands of others to do likewise.

Ursula Baatz has written a moving account of Enomiya-Lassalle—virtually unknown today but still relevant as a spiritual teacher for our fracturing age. Baatz tells Lassalle's life story in its human and fascinating detail. She shows how Lassalle saw a new consciousness emerging in the world but how his life focused not on abstractions, but on individual practice and direct experience—experience of the deep reality that unites all human beings. When so much political thinking is encased in notions of winning and competing, of them against us, nothing could be more timely than this heartfelt account.

Preface

H. Enomiya-Lassalle, SJ, was a bridge builder and peacemaker. He built the bridge between Zen Buddhism and Christianity, opening up a path that many follow today. He lived almost a century, from the end of the nineteenth century to his death at the end of the twentieth century. His life journey connected Europe with Asia and Christianity with Buddhism, as well as traditional Christian piety and theology with the non-Christian spiritual practice of the Zen tradition. A soldier in World War I, he survived the atomic bombing of Hiroshima. When he spoke of peace, he did so not with naivety but with the knowledge that true peace requires the ability to question oneself and to see things from others' perspectives. Peace requires a change in thinking, and the Zen practice he learned from Japanese Buddhist Zen masters offers an appropriate path to selflessness. Only when people transcend their personal, national, ethnic, and religious egotism can there be peace. Lassalle remained optimistic about this until the end of his life. Despite all the wars he had experienced, he considered the history of humanity to date as a path to greater peace, freedom, and justice. Human beings are designed to be happy, yet happiness lies only in that which does not change, not in that which changes. Buddhism, Christianity, and other religious traditions agree on this. Since human beings want to be happy, the pursuit of the "unborn and uncreated," as the Buddha calls it, will ultimately prevail as a "new consciousness."

The transformation that Lassalle initiated in Christian spirituality—not alone, but decisively—is most evident in a simple object: the meditation stool. Now found in nearly all Christian educational institutions and monasteries, the meditation stool first came to Europe from Japan in the 1960s via Lassalle. Until then, meditation and contemplation were practiced in the Christian context almost exclusively by a monastic elite. The Second Vatican Council (1962–1965) gave lay people a new position in the church and encouraged learning from the wisdom of other religions. Without the council, Lassalle's path would not have been possible. He was able to take advantage of the brief window of opportunity from the early 1960s to the late 1980s when an unprecedented openness to and between religions was possible. However, with the Islamic Revolution in Iran (1978–1979) and the pontificate of Pope John Paul II (1978–2005), these opportunities began to close.

Father Enomiya-Lassalle's life exemplifies the possibility of crossing the boundaries into other religions and cultures without losing one's own identity. His biography is an important and wholesome read because he repeatedly faced tremendous resistance but never lost courage.

November 2004

Note for the English Edition

Twenty years later, little seems to remain of the hope for a peaceful world that drove Father Lassalle. That is precisely why it is important, indeed vital, to continue on this path of deep peace and reconciliation between opposing forces.

Vienna, July 2025
Ursula Baatz

Acknowledgments

I would like to thank Professor Klaus Riesenhuber, SJ (Tokyo, 1938–2022) for initiating the "Lassalle Biography" project and my Zen teacher Ana Maria Schlüter Rodés (Zendo Betania, Brihuega/Spain) for her valuable feedback. Thanks also to Brigitte Voykowitsch (Vienna) for her helpful comments on the text and Karl Baier (Vienna) for terminological support. A special thanks to Jerry Brown, former governor of California, for making the English translation possible, and Dennis Johnson for translating the book.

1

The Pearl Diver

❧

He was tall and slender looking in the old black suit or the well-worn black cassock that came from the estate of a deceased fellow Jesuit. At first glance, despite his height, he seemed rather unassuming. Those who got to know him better quickly noticed the empathetic, tactful, but determined way he listened. Toward the end of his life, when his hearing was failing, he would cup his hands behind his ears to hear better. And somehow, when he listened in this way, with all his attention and devotion, the problems of others became more minor and bearable and sometimes disappeared altogether.

I was not the only one who came to know Father Hugo M. Enomiya-Lassalle in this way. The first time I saw him, he was passing through the dining room of the Mission House of St. Gabriel of the Society of the Divine Word in Mödling, near Vienna, in his worn cassock. Although obviously a priest, the man made a somewhat impoverished impression, and I thought someone should get him a new cassock. A little later, I realized that this man was the famous Father Lassalle, with whom I had taken a course in Zen.

This was in 1976, and Zen meditation—it would be better to say Zen contemplation—was the ultimate innovation for many people at the time. When it turned out that enlightenment did not set in after three sesshins, many were disappointed and did not return—but a large group did continue. Today, there is a Zen meditation group in almost every large city in Germany. Some are Buddhist, some are Christian, and many of the people who join them came to Zen in some way through Father Lassalle. Many have long years of practice under their belt, as more than sixty years have passed since Father Lassalle published his first book, *Zen: Way to Enlightenment*, a groundbreaking work that was translated into several languages.

Hugo Lassalle's connection between Christianity and Zen is unique from the perspective of the history of religions. Connections and exchanges between different religions have always existed because religions are not monolithic entities. For example, it can be shown that the practice of yoga has influenced the Jesus Prayer and the Prayer of the Heart of the Eastern Church[1] without compromising the Christian element. That a Christian can follow the path of Zen is possible only through and since the Second Vatican Council. The Council document *Nostra Aetate* (1965) states, "The Catholic Church rejects nothing that is true and holy in these religions. She regards with sincere reverence those ways of conduct and of life, those precepts and teachings which, though differing in many aspects from the ones she holds and sets forth, nonetheless often reflect a ray of that Truth which enlightens all men."[2] The Second Vatican Council not only opened the door to other religions and an openness to other cultures but also recommended integrating

---

[1] Karl Baier, *Yoga auf dem Weg nach Westen. Beiträge zur Rezeptionsgeschichte* (Königshausen & Neuman, 1998), chap. 4.
[2] *Nostra Aetate* § 2.

non-Christian spiritual practices. Religious institutions should reflect on "how Christian religious life might be able to assimilate the ascetic and contemplative traditions, whose seeds were sometimes planted by God in ancient cultures already prior to the preaching of the Gospel,"[3] says the Council document *Ad Gentes* (1965).

This paved the way for Hugo Lassalle and the Zen master Yamada Koun (1907–1989) to do something that had probably never been done before. Officials of the Christian churches—that is, Catholic priests and Protestant pastors—were granted some of the official authority of a Buddhist Zen master, but only those directly related to the practice of Zen. Yamada Koun Roshi considered everything related to the Buddhist religion—that is, rituals, vows, and even the title roshi—inappropriate for Christians. The only thing that mattered to Hugo Lassalle and Yamada Roshi, for different reasons, was "the teaching outside the scriptures that points directly to the human heart," as stated in Bodhidharma's famous stanza about Zen. These classical words translated in Father Lassalle's language: All people have the opportunity for "natural knowledge of God." For what can be realized about God is evident to all, says the Apostle Paul, and those who refuse to acknowledge this realization will be punished by being left to their passions. (Rom 1:19, 26). Hugo Lassalle set many things in motion. He played an important role in reviving Christian mysticism and contemplation. Many Christians in Europe, North America, South America, and Asia are now Zen teachers, Zen masters, or Zen practitioners thanks to his efforts. Above all, he helped many people experience God more deeply through his courses, books, and way of life.

---

[3] *Ad Gentes* §18.

Hugo Lassalle was a Jesuit to the core, completely commit-
ted to this way of life, and at the same time he was a seeker,
someone who was primarily
concerned with experiencing
the absolute and transforming
his own life.

Recognition within the
institutions—both the Roman
Catholic Church and Zen Buddhism—was important to him
because he was not only pursu-
ing a spiritual path for himself
but also wanted to provide a
sustainable path for others.

Those who knew him at the
end of his life had the impression of a person who had mas-
tered his life with sovereignty.

*Fr. Enomiya-Lassale in the 1970s, most
likely in Japan.*

This was true in a way, for he
was well aware of his doubts and weaknesses. His expression
was that of a man who had experienced much pain and who
had found peace at the bottom of that pain. And he hid that
aspect of himself as well. Then there was this old Jesuit who
was hard of hearing and forgetful, whose speech was slurred
and had old-fashioned views, who read Mass every day, prayed
the Breviary and the Rosary, and wore a large cross on the lapel
of his suit.

For many, the humility, lack of pretension, and the simplicity and naturalness with which Lassalle lived made him special.
"He radiated a certain something, and I thought to myself: I
must remember that. I won't see someone like that very often,"
said one person about Lassalle.

It was not until I read the approximately ten thousand pages
of Father Lassalle's handwritten notes, many of them written in

tiny letters and mainly in the old Sütterlin script, that I understood how hard-won this deep sense of peace was that radiated from him. That is probably why it was so convincing and helpful when people came to Father Lassalle with their difficulties, and he simply said, "That can happen sometimes. Just carry on."

This little book is an attempt to briefly summarize the most critical aspects of Hugo M. Enomiya-Lassalle's life. The quotes from the diary are in italics so that you can hear his own voice.

He was a master of Christian spirituality, meaning he followed the Zen path as a Christian who had a thorough training in Christian mysticism and spiritual practice. He came from nineteenth-century Catholicism, a form of piety that sought to separate and suppress the body and to promote thinking in concepts and prayer with words and concrete images. Mortification was an essential concept in the piety that Hugo Lassalle had learned. The practice of Zen required him to renounce just that: to open his senses and let go of conceptual thinking. The fact that Hugo Lassalle embarked on this path speaks to his courage and determination to follow the path of the mystics. It did not take him long to realize that Christian mysticism and Zen practice are closely related. "Letting go" and selflessness form the basis of both paths; and both agree that nothing can be said about the ultimate, about God, absolute reality, nirvana, etc. because all human language is limiting.

The courage to take a step again and again into an unknown horizon in the search for God was one of the defining characteristics of Lassalle's life. This gave hope to many people because they could see in him that aging and old age do not have to be synonymous with decrepitude and loss of vitality. He gave hope not only through what he said but simply by being who he was.

For Father Lassalle, Zen practice was not a form of individualistic spirituality or without ethics. He set clear standards but also knew that people need time to change. *Metanoia*, or trans-formation of the heart, was most important to him. His way of offering nondirective suggestions helped many people. Once, a woman said, her *dokusan* was about the fact that she had done something wrong but did not feel guilty about it. Lassalle's answer was simple: "I once met a swindler in Geneva who also had no bad conscience." "I still carry that with me today," says the woman, and it changed her life. Many others have had similar experiences. After one of his lectures in St. Peter's Church in Cologne in 1979, people approached Father Lassalle with further questions. A young man joined the group curiously. Lassalle looked at him. The young man, who was not the sensitive type, burst into tears and ran away to hide in the crowd. He later said that his life took a new direction as a result.

Another time, it must have been in 1985, there was a woman who often visited the meditation house St. Franziskus in Dietfurt in the Altmühltal, where Lassalle had a private room and where he held most of the sesshins in the last years of his life. She was in her fifties, had a well-paid position as a scientific officer, and had just decided to quit her job and move to the St. Franziskus Meditation House. Nobody knew about it except her. When she entered Lassalle's room that morning to bring him the mail, he said pretty unexpectedly, "Whatever one has decided to do, one should do." The woman was speechless. Then she really did move to Dietfurt.

For Lassalle, the practice of Zen was a contribution to world peace. He had lived through and survived two world wars, witnessed the end of European colonialism and the first stirrings of a global society, and experienced the nuclear threat of the Cold War. World peace requires a fundamental change in human consciousness, an end to thinking in terms of opposites and selfishness. He believed that the practice of contemplation paves the way to this new consciousness, and we are on the threshold of such a development. A peaceful world is possible. His views have often been associated with New Age and branded as unrealistic. However, such sudden shifts in the collective consciousness have occurred before. There is no other way to explain that at some point in the past, deceased rulers were no longer accompanied by real people, horses, etc. to serve them in the afterlife, but by figures and symbols—an enormous advance in abstraction. And after all, one of the hallmarks of Christianity is to expect the impossible, to hope against hope.

People, as Father Lassalle once said, have a deep inner experience of what they will one day become. This knowledge is like a seed. And just as a seed needs air, water, earth, and sun to become, for example, a rose, we humans need more than food and drink to become what we are. Everything is necessary, even difficulties and pain, in order to become what we truly are over time.

The *imitatio Christi,* the imitation of Christ, marked Lassalle's entire life. He did not talk much about it, but anyone who participated in Eucharist with him could notice that.

He occasionally told the story of the pearl seeker, the parable of the merchant and the pearl.

ॐ

Once upon a time, there was a merchant who dealt with pearls and jewels of all kinds. He was very wealthy and traveled extensively, buying the finest gems and the most brilliant pearls here and there and selling them at a good profit. He was not only a talented merchant but also a lover of the fire in the gems and the shimmering luster of the pearls, and as such, he was highly esteemed by connoisseurs in his field. One day, he was presented with a very special pearl. It had something that set it apart from all the other pearls; perhaps it was the luster, or maybe it was the shape, or perhaps it was a little of everything. The merchant saw the pearl and was deeply moved by its absolute beauty. He could hardly take his eyes off this jewel, but he turned pale when he asked for its price. It was more than he had ever paid for any gem or pearl. He quickly counted his possessions and realized that he could only buy the pearl if he sold everything he owned, and that was a lot. But he could not forget the pearl. It attracted him like a candle attracts a moth, irresistibly, until the moth burns in the flame. The merchant decided to sell everything to have that one pearl. He knew that this was sheer madness in the eyes of his acquaintances and customers and that he would own nothing but the pearl, but he didn't care. He paid what was asked for the pearl, left everything he had ever owned, and disappeared from the lives of the people who had known him. He no longer interacted with them, instead living as a beggar on the fringes of society, sometimes stretching out his hand for alms, sometimes gratefully accepting a piece of bread. He had carefully hidden the pearl under his rags, and no one knew of the treasure he carried above his heart. But many who met him and gave him money, food, or a kind look felt a deep joy and great peace emanating from the beggar.

☙

"And again, the kingdom of heaven is like a pearl . . ." The story of the merchant who sold everything to possess this one pearl is in the Gospel of Matthew (13:45–46) and Father Lassalle often shared it in his Zen classes. He would say that people thought the merchant was crazy, but in fact, he lacked nothing because he had the pearl. Perhaps it is no coincidence that the parable of the pearl is found in the Gospels as well as in Gnostic and Buddhist texts; the pearl is always the symbol of the absolute. The point is that the pearl is so incomparable and precious that one must be willing to sacrifice everything to possess it, but having it makes one infinitely happy and free. According to the Sermon on the Mount, it is about attaining perfection: "You should therefore be perfect, just as your heavenly Father is perfect, for he causes the sun to rise on the good and the evil and the rain to fall on the just and the unjust" (Mt 5:45, 48). In Buddhist terms, it is the realization of one's Buddha nature, where realization means both understanding and actual embodiment.

It is not surprising that the story of the pearl is found in various religious traditions. The story touches on the depths of human existence, where we come from and where we are going, and what to do with the few decades that make up a human life. When it comes to life and death, our personal and existential choices are no longer determined by dogmas and answers that may be right in one system and wrong in another. Faced with the inevitability of death, each person's life reflects their ability to live authentically, that is, to integrate death into their lives.

Father Hugo M. Enomiya-Lassalle was a living example of how to live with the certainty of one's mortality. He was not afraid of death, and what came after was an open question for him. In the first seconds after the atomic bomb exploded in Hiroshima, his first thought was that now he would know what lies beyond death. But he survived the blast. *Since I have received the gift of life again, I will do everything with renewed strength for my own development and for the salvation of souls,*[4] he wrote in his diary. For this reason, in 1956, at fifty-eight years, Father Lassalle began intensive Zen practice in a Buddhist monastery in Japan—at an age when other people are planning their retirement. What he was looking for was the experience of God. For, as he said, *the only sadness is not to be a saint.*[5]

Hugo M. Enomiya-Lassalle is one of the greatest spiritual

---

[4] September 18, 1945 (for diary entries only the date is shown).
[5] October 18, 1945.

bridge-builders of the twentieth century, one of those rare people who dare to cross from one culture and religion to another without abandoning their own tradition. Many people are still irritated by the fact that Father Lassalle, as a Jesuit and Catholic priest, practiced and later taught Buddhist meditation. That is a risky thing to do, because you have to put your own identity on the line, but then, of course, you find a new, larger, and deeper view of yourself and the world. Father Lassalle did not choose the path of Zen out of dissatisfaction with Christianity. He had come to Japan as a Catholic missionary. He wanted to know the deeper dimensions of Japanese culture through Zen practice and find a way of prayer suitable for Japanese Christians. In the process, he discovered that the practice of Zen was helpful in his search for God. "God" should not remain a concept but become an experience.

The great Chinese Zen master Joshu (778–897) once compared himself to a bridge: it is there for everyone, for the wise and the foolish, for the good and the bad, for animals and humans—everyone can cross it.[6] Father Lassalle was such a bridge, a bridge of hope.

---

[6] Hekiganroku Nr. 52.

2

The Call of the Cuckoo

🌢

The religious wars between Christian denominations that ravaged Europe from the sixteenth to the mid-eighteenth centuries cost tens of millions of lives. And until the 1960s, belonging to a Catholic or Protestant denomination determined living conditions and social opportunities. It is perhaps no wonder that dialogue and reconciliation between religions was so important to Father Lassalle: the religious wars played a decisive role in his family's history.

Father Lassalle's ancestors were Huguenots, members of the Protestant minority in France who escaped persecution by the Catholic king in 1699 and fled from France to Germany. They were craftsmen, worked in the textile industry, and were among the founders of the Huguenot town of Karlshafen. But when one of the descendants of the Protestant refugees married a Catholic, he had to agree to have his children raised as Catholics. As Hugo Lassalle later remarked with a particular grin, the Protestant Lassalles became Catholics in Protestant Germany and thus again belonged to a religious minority in northern Germany, this time the Catholics. The Lassalles settled in Catholic Hildesheim, a Catholic enclave in the Protestant Kingdom of Hanover. Craftsmen and small business owners like the Lassalles dominated daily life. Hildesheim was a small town without any significant structural changes since the Middle Ages. To this day, a sense of this different way of life can be felt in the old half-timbered buildings that survived the bombing of World War II.

At the beginning of the nineteenth century, industrialization began in Prussia, more precisely in Silesia, the Ruhr area, and the capital Berlin. The gray coal smoke that settled everywhere in the new industrial areas symbolizes this era. The steam engine powered the latest means of transportation, the locomotive, and above all, the machines that made mass production possible for the first time.

In 1835, when the first railway line in Germany went into operation, Franz Bernhard Lassalle, a member of the fifth generation of the Huguenot family, was sixteen years old. The rise of the Lassalle family began with this young apprentice tailor. The young tailor felt restless in the quiet town of Hildesheim. After a few years of travel, which took him to Paris, where he is said to have earned his money as a claqueur at the opera, and probably also to England, where the first wave of industrialization had already passed its peak, Franz Bernhard Lassalle settled in Berlin in 1850. Considering that at that time there were only forty-seven cities in all of Europe with more than 100,000 inhabitants, Berlin, with a population of almost half a million, was a large city. The outskirts of Berlin were still rural, but an industrial belt was already developing around the city.

Franz Bernhard and a partner set up shop in the center, on Behrenstraße, a side street near today's Französische Straße subway station. In their men's tailoring shop, a bolt of the finest cloth was displayed in the window, and when an order came in, the necessary fabric was initially purchased on credit. At the time, Berlin was the capital of the emerging industrial and military nation of Prussia. The military dominated the streets and society in many ways, so a clever and swift tailor could make a good living. In 1870, Lassalle & Zürcher was awarded the title of "Purveyor to the Court of His Royal Highness Prince Frederick Carl of Prussia." Members of the higher nobility and the Prussian officer corps had their uniforms measured here. Up to eighty seamstresses were employed in the now large business, making insignia, epaulets, etc. and sewing them onto the Prussian blue cloth. The poor tailor had become a member of the upper class of Wilhelmine Berlin, whose vote in the Reichstag elections counted as much as that of a hundred poor workers.

But Franz Bernhard Lassalle seems to have been drawn back to Hildesheim. He bought a large piece of land on the Moritzberg, which is now part of Hildesheim. The manor house he built, which is still very impressive today, included a kitchen, an orchard, and stables for horses, cows, sheep, and pigs. In other words, the Lassalles had become landowners and self-sufficient, a status that meant wealth and prestige.

Franz Bernhard left his nine children more than half a million gold marks when he died. (At that time, the average annual income of a worker was between 700 and 1,200 marks). Georg Lassalle, the youngest of the family, rented a mansion in Externbrock, Westphalia, with the intention of making a living in agriculture, after graduating from high school and completing a status-appropriate year of service in the military where one is discharged as a reserve officer. That same year, 1896, he married Elisabeth Feltmann; the following year their first son, Bernhard, was born, and a year later, in 1898, Hugo Lassalle was born.

By this time, however, the agricultural era was coming to an end. International trade increased, and protective tariffs were introduced in Prussia to prevent cheap grain imports from the US and Eastern Europe. When these tariffs were lifted in 1895, agriculture was in crisis. Georg Lassalle, who had clearly misjudged the situation, was forced to give up the estate. The family moved to Göttingen, where Georg Lassalle studied law from 1900 to 1903. Then they returned to Hildesheim. The family moved into a newly built house in the best part of town. It was here that Bernhard and Hugo grew up, as well as Hans, the mentally disabled brother born in 1900, and the two sisters Maria (1901) and Elisabeth (1908).

A childhood photograph shows Hugo Lassalle in a sailor's suit, which was fashionable for little boys at the time—a reference to the militaristic era, as the German navy was the pride of the empire. Apart from his brother's mental disability, which must have had a profound effect on the two-year-old Hugo, even if he didn't talk about it, he seems to have had a sheltered and relatively carefree childhood. Their parents seem to have been as strict as was customary at the time, which meant that they occasionally used corporal punishment. On the other hand, the children enjoyed a great deal of freedom, "more than children today," as Hugo Lassalle sometimes remarked during lectures. School does not seem to have been a particular problem for Hugo. He learned to play the cello at a maternal uncle's music school, an instrument he loved and occasionally played during his early years in Japan until his cello was incinerated in the inferno of the atomic bombing of Hiroshima.

From an early age, children were taught and trained in the main virtues of the bourgeois work ethic: regularity, punctuality, and duty. Although Hugo Lassalle was obviously a socially well-adjusted child, and his behavior and academic performance met expectations, he found *no satisfaction* in this kind of work. He was thirteen and in high school when that nagging feeling of dissatisfaction first appeared,[1] and it would remain with him throughout his life, no matter how successful he was outwardly.

Little Hugo was taught to pray by his mother, Elisabeth,

---

[1] March 9, 1968.

whose maiden name was Feltmann. She came from a decidedly Catholic family. Her great-uncle Hugo Feltmann had been vicar general in Hildesheim and had acted as mediator in the disputes between the Catholic Church and the Prussian state during the Bismarck era. Her brother, who was called Hugo Feltmann, was also a priest and the cathedral vicar of Hildesheim, holding from 1906 a leading position in the then-new church institution Caritas. He was the godfather of Hugo Lassalle. He was a sociable man and a cigar smoker, as shown in a family photo from 1951. And it was probably he who took the ten or twelve-year-old Hugo to the Sarrasani Circus. Here, Hugo Lassalle saw for the first time Japanese in the flesh. "They were doing a pike dive through a long wire tube. I can still see one of the Japanese standing there—and 'pfft,'—he was already through the tube. After that, the jump was made more difficult by a man with a sword or knife stabbing through the wire."[2] The scene was still vivid before the ninety-year-old's eye. For a Catholic family in northern Germany, the Lassalles were quite atypical: they were wealthy and educated, in contrast to the average German Catholic, who belonged to the lower class regarding income and education. Georg Lassalle was also politically active. He was a member of the influential Catholic Center Party. All of this suggests that the Lassalle family was Catholic, socially engaged, and open to contemporary issues.

As a schoolboy, Hugo became an altar boy and met a Jesuit for the first time. The Jesuit order was banned in Germany after Bismarck's Kulturkampf. Jesuits were only allowed to preach on special occasions, such as "the Volksmission." The young altar boy was impressed by the strange preacher. "I want to be

---

[2] "Die Entdeckung des Zen-Weges, Ein Gespräch mit Pater Dr. Hugo M. Enomiya-Lassalle," in Übung *der Kontemplation: Christen gehen den Zen-Weg*, ed. Günter Stachel (Matthias-Grünewald-Verl, 1988), 10.

a Jesuit, too," he said. "Don't you dare do something stupid like that," said the priest, Hugo Lassalle told us with a smile as an old Jesuit.[3]

Then came 1914. The general enthusiasm for war also gripped the men of the Lassalle family. The father, Georg and the elder brother Bernhard wanted to enlist immediately, but their mother dissuaded them. Perhaps it was her religious attitude that made her skeptical about the enthusiasm for war, or maybe it was a realistic assessment of the situation; at the beginning of the war, no one thought that the war would last long and that there would be many deaths. Hugo Lassalle was drafted in 1916 and was sent to Potsdam to join the guard because of his height. There, they did drills and practiced target shooting. In his diary, he laconically noted his progress in hitting the target and the addresses of new friends among the recruits. His brother Bernhard, who had been drafted before him, was wounded on the Eastern Front. When he recovered, he was transferred to the Western Front. "Here he came under heavy fire, a grenade exploded near him, and he had to be taken to the military hospital with a serious wound. Since we always had an excellent relationship, he let me know that he didn't know if he was going to make it. When I was about to leave, I was told that he had already overcome the danger of death."[4] Yet, weakened by the severe head injury, Bernhard died of pneumonia in the spring of 1917. A blow that deeply affected the younger brother.

Hugo Lassalle was also transferred to the Western Front, where the deadly trench warfare was literally devouring young Germans and Frenchmen. During the summer and fall of 1917, Hugo Lassalle was stationed near Reims and repeat-

---

[3] Reported by Fr. Johannes Kopp SAC.
[4] Hugo M. Enomiya-Lassalle, *Mein Weg zum Zen* (Kösel-Verlag, 2018), 14 (hereinafter MWZ).

edly involved in heavy fighting. The entries in his diaries from this period are written in Gabelsberger shorthand and could not be deciphered. But they reveal the pressure and haste of those days. In the fall, Hugo Lassalle, now a private, was wounded. "In October, I was sent with a patrol to a relatively quiet place to take prisoners and interrogate them about the positions of the enemy troops. I was specially trained for this and joined an assault team. After two of my comrades were killed, I was wounded in the foot. It wasn't a severe wound, an embedded bullet, but because it was in the ankle, it took a long time to heal."[5] He received the Iron Cross the day after he was wounded. At the end of his life, in his reticent way, he explained that, unlike his older brother, he had been lucky: "Actually, I was almost never in close combat, with the exception of this patrol, where I also threw a grenade, which probably killed the person who shot at me."[6]

His injury prevented him from being sent back to the front and probably saved his life. On the Western Front, in the spring of 1918, the German General Staff again tried to reverse the "bad luck" of the Central Powers. The young, mostly inexperienced soldiers died in regiments; for example, in front of Langenmarck, but also elsewhere. Later, they were hailed as heroes. Hugo Lassalle was indeed lucky.

It was around this time, in February 1918, that he was able to take the war matriculation examination, having been in the military hospital at Brilon in the Sauerland region since Christmas 1917. With the exception of geography and history, he received a "sufficient" in all subjects. The examiner found his final essay on the horrors of war too objective. "In all times, war has been a terrible misery. Because in war, a lot of blood is shed, and wide, blooming swaths of land are devastated. Sol-

---

[5] MWZ, 14.
[6] MWZ, 15.

diers become very brutal and don't care about right and wrong as long as they don't violate their laws of war . . . But there has never been a war as terrible as this one." And with sober words, Hugo Lassalle listed the effects of modern war technology. But behind the objectivity, the horror resonates. "The projectiles used today are sometimes very large and therefore naturally have a tremendous effect. Even shrapnel from medium-sized shells can fly several hundred meters and cause terrible wounds due to the enormous pressure. Relatively small shrapnel can tear off an entire limb. If a grenade explodes near a person, there is usually nothing left of him."[7] His personal experience is packaged in sentences that sound detached but vibrate with the depth of emotion.

Decades later, in 1973, the then seventy-five-year-old described his time in the field as the happiest of his life: *I realized that my three happiest periods were 1) the time in the field during World War I, 2) the novitiate, 3) the tertianship [. . .] not only in terms of time, but also in terms of intensity, in the same order. If I could hope for an intensification, it would perhaps be a conclusion in the Carthusian monastery.*[8]

It sounds absurd to compare war with the two Jesuit "intensive courses" at the beginning and end of the preparation for entering the order. But there is a similarity between the constant proximity to death in war and the process of novitiate and tertianship. In all three cases, it is a matter of letting go of the self and all that has become dear to one's heart and dying into a greater life. For Hugo Lassalle, the movement of the heart toward God is the substance of his life. And it seems that the proximity of death in the war brought about a similarly intense opening of the heart as his time in the novitiate and later in the tertianship.[9]

---

[7] MWZ, 17.
[8] March 3, 1973.
[9] Tertianship is the final stage of formation for Jesuits before taking final vows. It involves apostolic work and spiritual renewal, including a thirty-day

The war had shattered old values and orders, both political and religious. Hugo Lassalle's brother and many friends had died on the battlefields. "We were very depressed after the war. This situation went hand in hand with a strong religious movement,"[10] he said later. Then, he read the life of Ignatius of Loyola (1491–1556), the founder of the Jesuits. The path of the young Spanish courtier and officer, motivated by honor and recognition, who became a "soldier of God" after his injury, moved the former soldier Hugo Lassalle. *I remember [. . .] that reading the biography, which I did at the end of the war (1918), made me realize what a saint is.*[11] He decided to follow the example of Ignatius and become a Jesuit. On April 25, 1919, Hugo Lassalle entered the novitiate of the Jesuits in s'-Heerenberg in the Netherlands.

The situation in Germany after World War I was politically and socially turbulent and unstable. Inflation robbed many families, including the Lassalles, of their wealth, and hunger was the norm. The Treaty of Versailles, which left the Germans with no opportunities for development, laid the groundwork for deep discontent and growing militancy. Hugo Lassalle was hardly aware of all this.

After entering the novitiate, he kept his civilian clothes for the first three weeks, after which he received the black habit of the order, the collar, and the belt that went with it. A rosary, a book with the rules of the Society of Jesus, and a large crucifix were also part of the novice's equipment. The days were strictly regulated. Awake at five-thirty, then first a reflective prayer ("Betrachtung"),[12] then Mass, after breakfast a reflec-

---

retreat based on the Spiritual Exercises of St. Ignatius.

[10] MWZ, 15.

[11] March 9, 1983.

[12] "Betrachtung" is close to the medieval "meditation." For the English translation of "Betrachtung" as "discursive prayer," see Augustin Poulain, SJ, *The Graces of Interior Prayer* (1910) (thanks to Karl Baier for the note).

tion on the first reflective prayer, then work in the garden or in the house. After that, the novice master gave instructions, and before lunch, there was a reading from *The Imitation of Christ* by Thomas à Kempis (1380–1471)[13]; lunch came with a table reading; then recreation, that is, a period of rest followed by time for personal reading; coffee at four o'clock; another reflective prayer before dinner; and recreation after dinner. At the end of the day, the novice master would explain the reflective prayer for the next morning, and immediately before going to bed, the novice would kneel before the statue of Mary in the chapel and pray the "Memorare" of Bernard of Clairvaux (1090–1153), a consecration to Mary, Queen of Heaven. The daily routine was strictly divided into small units, and acoustic signals indicated the beginning and end of each section. In this way, the individual was gradually integrated into an order and a way of life in which he could find his new identity as a Jesuit.

The first major thirty-day retreat, the Ignatian Exercises, was crucial. It was during these weeks that the novice had to discern if the decision to become a Jesuit was the right one and if he was truly called to live his life as a religious and a member of the Society of Jesus. The goal of the Ignatian Exercises is always the same: to give life the right direction. The goal of life is God, and once that is realized, all other circumstances in life fall into place around that goal, like iron filings around a magnet. Whether someone has a vocation to religious life is secondary in this sense. Nevertheless, religious orders have been and still are considered a kind of elite of Christian life. Its members should live exemplary lives, and their vows of poverty, chastity, and obedience make them people who try to live as selfless a life as possible. Yet holiness is not a privilege of the religious alone.

---

[13] *De Imitatione Christi* (c. 1418–1427) by Thomas à Kempis is a handbook for the spiritual life of the Devotio Moderna, a spiritual movement focusing on personal experience. It influenced the Ignatian Exercises and is still a widely read classic.

In any case, the first step on this path is an insight into one's bad habits and the goodness of God. The Exercises start with these reflective prayers and examinations, and afterward the life of Jesus offers a wealth of scenes in which one can immerse oneself with all senses to gain insights that will shape one's own life.

One meditation in particular attracted Hugo Lassalle. Lucifer, the prince of devils, sits on a throne of smoke and fire and gathers his followers under the standard, or banner, of evil. He promises riches and glory, and his followers are proud and arrogant. Christ, on the other hand, gathers his followers in a humble but beautiful and graceful place. Those who serve him can expect poverty and slander, which must be endured with humility. One should visualize this scene as tangibly as possible and then choose under which lord and standard one would like to serve—under the standard of Lucifer and pride or the standard of Christ and humility.

The image obviously spoke to the former front-line soldier. Perhaps this was also so because he had been disillusioned by the collapse of the prewar world and the death of his brother Bernhard, which thus revealed the hollowness of the ideal of serving a secular ruler. Instead of the Emperor, there was now Christ the King, and the young Hugo Lassalle wanted to be an outstanding soldier of Christ: *What attracted me to Ignatius from the very beginning was the idea of distinguishing myself among my fellow human beings in the service of the King, Christ, in the Kingdom of God, and especially the transfer from the political "Emperor and Empire" to the spiritual Eternal King was very appealing.*[14]

For the young Jesuit, the battle had shifted to another level. It was no longer against an external enemy, but against himself, against his own "disordered desires" and his own selfish-

---

[14] June 6, 1974.

ness. Self-denial and asceticism were the means of this battle. The point was to orient one's whole life to God. According to a widespread belief among Christians, but not found in the Bible, the evil that dwells in the human soul prevents people from doing this. A popular spiritual manual of the time said, "We must be determined to watch over ourselves, to not let ourselves go, to be violent with ourselves, because otherwise we will not be able to cope with the disordered passions and with the evil that is in us and that always threatens and pursues us."[15] The fight against evil thus becomes a monumental effort to deprive sensuality of its substance in every form. In a sense, however, this was like throwing the baby out with the bathwater, for here selfishness and "disordered desires and passions" are confused with sensuality, that is, the ability to perceive with all the senses. In Hugo Lassalle's Zen practice, this idea of fighting sensuality proved to be an obstacle that was very difficult for him to overcome. Only gradually did he learn to trust his senses.

However, the decisive motive of Father Lassalle's life was not about being "against" but "for"; he was not defined by the fight against evil but by his unwavering progress on the path to God, and in this way he strove to become a saint. This is a fundamental motif of the spirituality of Ignatius of Loyola. *The following applies to progress: quantum exiverit* [how much one has stepped out of one's own will and self-interest] . . . *this must be considered in all sensual pleasures, so the more one renounces them, the better for one's progress,*[16] writes Father Lassalle. Spiritual progress leads to God, and that means home. For a saint finds God not only after death in the afterlife but already here and now, in the *visio beatifica*, the blissful vision of God. This is Christian tradition from the beginning. Hugo

---

[15] Maurice Meschler, *Aszese und Mystik* (Herder, 1917), 98ff.
[16] December 19, 1945.

Lassalle wants to become a saint in order to "see God as He is." This is the goal that Hugo Lassalle pursues throughout his life, and this motive also drives the practice of Zen.

The methods of Jesuit education helped to avoid certain mistakes along the way and overcome problems. For example, every novice had a string of beads, and every time he found himself in an action or thought that should be discarded, he pulled one of the beads. In this way, a certain mastery over thoughts, words, and actions could be achieved. There was also a so-called "guardian angel," another novice or cleric, who had to inform his "protégé" of his faults at specific intervals. During this early period in the Society, Father Hubert Hartmann, the novice master, was a formative influence on Hugo Lassalle. Father Hartmann's reliability in helping people in difficulty, even if it cost him much time and effort, and his deep piety must have left a lasting impression on Hugo Lassalle.

Hugo Lassalle's greatest problem throughout his life was what he called his "fear of people"—the fear of being rejected by others, whether in an exam situation, a public lecture, or a conflict that forced him to expose himself. The novice master, Father Hartmann, advised him, *"If you want to overcome the fear of people, you must seek contempt,"*[17] and Hugo Lassalle followed this recommendation throughout his life. In the many situations in his life when his self-esteem suffered, he adhered to the advice on the "third degree of humility" in the Ignatian Exercises. Father Hartmann had pointed this out to him in a confession during his novitiate.

The first degree of humility is to subordinate one's own will to God's law, which one always tries to follow. The second degree of humility is indifference to the things of the world and to one's own life, provided that "it does not interfere with the service of God our Lord." The third degree of humility goes

---

[17] October 10, 1974.

one step further and seeks "to follow Christ our Lord ever more closely and to become more like him in deeds." One strives more and more to wish for poverty and disgrace in community with the "poor Christ," and one longs more and more "to be considered a fool and a madman for Christ's sake."[18]

Hugo Lassalle sought to follow the path of the fool who, blinded by love, does not seek public recognition or approval because his only goal is Christ. *In the desire to attain Christ, to throw everything away, in a sense blind to the disadvantages that arise from wanting to attain Christ alone. Nothing else matters.*[19]

In this deep love, Hugo Lassalle lost himself more and more in the person of Christ. *Cum Christo crucifixus sum cruci: Non iam ego vivo sed Christus vivit in me.*[20] With Christ, I am crucified, and "it is no longer I who live but Christ lives in me." This phrase from the Apostle Paul (Gal 2:20) was the defining maxim of Hugo Lassalle's life. What began in the novitiate was completed through the practice of Zen.

Actually, the young Jesuit wanted to go as a missionary to Africa to help the lepers there. So he wrote to the Superior General in Rome. "I received a direct reply from Father General saying that it was not God's will for me to go to Africa and thanking me for volunteering for Japan," he later said.[21] The course was set, although the future missionary still had seven years of study ahead of him.

The Jesuit study house in Valkenburg in the Dutch province of Limburg, like the novitiate in 's-Heerenberg, was unusually modern for the time. It had coke central heating, electric light, and electric machines in the kitchen and workshops. The

---

[18] *The Spiritual Exercises of Ignatius of Loyola*, no. 67.
[19] February 7, 1950.
[20] February 1, 1950.
[21] "Zen and Christianity in Encounter," interview by Ruben Habito with Yamada Roshi and Fr. Enomiya-Lassalle, unpublished manuscript. See also Stachel, "Die Entdeckung des Zen-Weges," 9.

building was made of reinforced concrete, but the neo-Gothic pointed arches made it look like a medieval monastery. The small room into which Hugo Lassalle moved as a student was sparsely furnished: a desk, a chair, a kneeling bench, a bed with a nightstand, and a wardrobe with a built-in washbasin. This remained the standard for the rest of a Jesuit's life. As in the novitiate, life was strictly regulated. One got up at half past five, and most of the time was devoted to study. Hugo Lassalle was not an enthusiastic student, but his *religious conviction and willpower*[22] helped him get through his studies.

It was during his first year in Valkenburg that Hugo Lassalle was *suddenly* deeply moved in the dining room. A *touch* that was *a deeper and sweeter comfort* than anything he was to receive later. This experience set the course for his whole life. *At that time, I called it the call of the cuckoo.*[23] [. . .] *For a long time after that, this relived in memory occasionally, but it became rarer and weaker until it disappeared completely . . . the longing remains,*[24] he wrote later. Longing, but also *untroubled joy*, gave depth and direction to his life. The strength he drew from it also helped him to endure the long periods of study.

Both the three-year study of philosophy and the subsequent four-year study of theology were based on neo-Scholasticism. This school of thought emerged in the second half of the nineteenth century and was the binding foundation for all Catholic theologians. Its model was Thomas Aquinas, one of the most influential thinkers in the Western world. The Dominican friar, who taught philosophy in Paris in the thirteenth century, had become acquainted with the ancient Greek philosopher Aristotle through transmissions and translations from the Islamic world. This was a great challenge for the theologian,

---

[22] May 5, 1953.
[23] July 4, 1970.
[24] June 4, 1970.

for how could unbiased and reasoned thought be reconciled with the faith demanded by the Bible as a revelatory scripture? Thomas found a highly creative solution that laid the foundation for all subsequent Western theology. Seven hundred years later, neo-Thomism tried to bring this creative solution back into the picture. Meanwhile, the thinkers of the Enlightenment and the new natural sciences were dissecting the ancient worldview, and with this the authority of the magisterium of the church was challenged. How could modern science and the modern world be reconciled with the Christian faith and Catholic tradition? One attempt to solve the problem was to make neo-Thomism the binding norm for all thought within the Catholic Church.

For neo-Scholasticism, it seemed that God could be explained as a concept through deductions and proofs based on logical laws. Even though the Valkenburg professors dealt with modern philosophy—with Kant or Heidegger, for example—their train of thought always ended up with neo-scholastic reasoning.

The language of instruction was Latin. Not only were the textbooks written in Latin, but Latin was also spoken—for example, in the "disputations," in which two students each had to debate a dogmatic topic in front of an audience. The ability to argue clearly and conclusively was highly valued. The prospective Jesuits also attended lectures on psychology, physics, and biology. In the natural sciences, the program was up to date. The biology professor, for example, taught a moderate Darwinism, which was not at all common at the time. The theory of human descent from apes was still controversial, not only within the church but also outside of it. The Jesuit university was also very progressive in matters of social ethics, and one of Hugo Lassalle's fellow students, Oswald von Nell-Breuning, became one of the most important social ethicists of the Catholic Church in the twentieth century. Both the trade union movement in Germany and the postwar Adenauer government sought his advice.

A small detail shows how important social issues were to Hugo Lassalle. Among the large boxes in which his estate was stored was a series of postcards entitled "Voices of God and Voices of Our Time," woodcuts depicting the social misery and unemployment of the 1920s. Father Lassalle kept these postcards even in Japan and for more than seventy years.

To prepare for his work in Japan, the young Jesuit studied books about the sixteenth-century Japanese mission of Saint Francis Xavier. And, he later said, he practiced sitting on the floor in the unfamiliar position described in missionary texts. Among the international community of Jesuit students in Valkenburg were two Japanese, Aloysius Ogihara, who later became Bishop of Hiroshima, and Franz Xaver Abe, so Father Lassalle did not have to rely on books alone for his studies of Japan.

Hugo Lassalle was a model for his fellow students in his seriousness and desire to use all his energies as a missionary. On August 28, 1927, Lassalle was ordained priest with his friend Bruno Bitter. The sincere earnestness with which he knelt and prayed in the chapel on the eve of his ordination left a lasting impression on the younger men. The months that followed were again crucial for the young priest. He was not yet a Jesuit in the complete sense of the word, for he had yet to take his final vows. To prepare for that, his superiors sent him to France for a tertianship with the Jesuit Louis Poullier (1865–1940), who had been to China and had experience in missionary work in the Far East. More importantly, Father Poullier was knowledgeable about mysticism, had first-hand experience, and was considered a saint.

During these months of his tertianship, nothing distracted Hugo Lassalle from his path of prayer and intense devotion to God. It is man's destiny to be happy, Ignatius taught, and this happiness is not to be found in transitory things, but only in the immutable, in God. This is the classical theological tradition. In the tertianship, this formula took on a new dimension for Hugo Lassalle. Father Poullier taught that the goal of the Christian life is not only to be oriented to the imperishable but to achieve a mystical union with the imperishable, with God. For Louis Poullier, however, there was no contradiction between mystical practice and everyday ecclesiastical and institutional life. He was obviously an intense person. "His spiritual radiance and joyful love, his union with God, and his poverty are certainly attested,"[25] it is said of him. The fact that he stipulated in his will that all his writings should be burned after his death also shows how radical he was in his demands on himself.

Through Father Poullier, Hugo Lassalle became acquainted with the writings of the great Spanish mystics Teresa of Ávila (1515–1582) and John of the Cross (1542–1591), who later served as his guides in the world of Zen practice. This form of training including mysticism was an innovation of the Jesuits. Although the tertiate had always been a "school of the affections" and a guide to inner prayer, it was during these early years of the twentieth century that "a fundamental, systematic introduction to mysticism was given for the first time" in the tertiate, according to the memoirs of the German Jesuit priest Friedrich Muckermann (1883–1946).[26] Since the end of the nineteenth century, interest in mysticism had grown so much among the so-called "simple believers," the laity, that the clergy sometimes warned against mysticism.[27] The writings of Meister Eckhart, newly translated from Middle High German,

---

[25] Marcel Viller, Charles Baumgartner, and André Rayez, eds., *Dictionnaire de spiritualite ascetique et mystique* (G. Beauchesne et ses fils, 1932), 12:2035f (hereinafter DS).

[26] Friedrich Muckermann, SJ, *Im Kampf zwischen den Epochen: Lebenserinnerungen* (Matthias-Grünewald, 1973), 201.

[27] *Cf.*, e.g., Meschler, *Aszese und Mystik*, 186f.

as well as the first translation of the Discourses of Buddha, were bestsellers in the years following the First World War.

Louis Poullier's practical instructions aimed at learning to distinguish between the various feelings and states of mind that overwhelm one during the day and especially during prayer. Above all, one should pay attention to the joyful impulses that come from the depths of the soul. Attention to these "consolations" creates an appetite for "heavenly things." The consolations, Poullier wrote, foster "repugnance to the things of this world," and thus bring liberation from vices; "at the same time, it [the consolation] leads positively to God, and makes the path that leads to him enticing: under its guidance, the soul has the desire and the strength to go, yes, to run, to the heights of prayer and virtue."[28] The doctrine of consolations can be found in detail in the writings of the ancient Christian theologian Diadochus of Photike (d. 486), which became the official manual for novice masters of the Society of Jesus in the sixteenth century, and it was appropriated by St. Ignatius in his Spiritual Exercises. The second authoritative work was *The Imitation of Christ* by Thomas à Kempis, written in the fifteenth century and still widely read today. "Everything that is not God is nothing and must be regarded as nothing"; this is the basic instruction. This sense of radicalism corresponded to the young Jesuit Hugo Lassalle's longing for the experience of God, which had been burning within him since the "call of the cuckoo." Marked *by the once-ignited fire of divine love, or rather by the wound of love that could no longer heal and demanded total renunciation,*[29] he strove for the Grail, for union with God.

---

[28] Louis Poullier, "Consolation spirituel," in *Dictionnaire de spiritualité, ascétique et mystique, doctrine et histoire*, vol XII/2, 1624.
[29] December 19, 1945.

3

In the Land
of the Rising Sun

❧

Father Hugo Lassalle arrived in Japan on October 3, 1929, a week before the infamous Black Friday, when the New York stock market crashed. Japan was to become his home, for missionaries were not seasonal workers; they stayed abroad for a long time, often for the rest of their lives.

Japan, "the land of the rising sun," had captured the imagination of Europeans in many ways since the mid-nineteenth century. On the one hand, there was the story of the beautiful Japanese woman with a lung disease who falls in love with a European—the subject of Puccini's opera *Madame Butterfly*. On the other hand, there was the slogan of the Prussian King Wilhelm II about the "yellow peril" that threatened Europe. Little was known about the island nation on the other side of the globe. The objects of art and everyday use that came to Europe during the two Worlds' Fairs in Paris in 1867 and 1878 fueled exotic fantasies. For example, artists, such as van Gogh, were heavily influenced by Japanese art. Meanwhile, in Japan, there was a desire to acquire the knowledge and technical skills of Europeans and Americans. For over three hundred years, the island nation had been almost completely isolated from outside influences and pursued its own development. Firearms, for example, which had been brought to Japan by the first Europeans, were banned. The few conflicts that occurred were fought with traditional weapons. When the gunboats of the US Colonel Perry appeared off the coast of Osaka in 1853, Japan lacked the means to defend itself. The country was forced to open itself to foreigners and serve as a base for American ships. After the fall of the samurai regime—the shoguns had ruled from 1192 to 1868—Japan modernized at a tremendous pace under the Meiji ruler. The old class distinctions and privileges of the samurai were abolished, industrialization was promoted, and postal services, railways, and Western science and technology were introduced. By 1905, just fifty years later, after its victory in the Russo-Japanese War, Japan had become the leading power in the Pacific region.

Similar to what is happening in emerging Asian markets today, Japan was a country where cutting-edge technology met an ancient rural culture. There were high-rise buildings in the cities, while in the countryside, farmers lived in their traditional houses. City dwellers wore Western clothes, but the traditional kimono still dominated the streetscape. By the beginning of the twentieth century, a consumer culture had developed, with large department stores as its centerpiece. The Japanese film industry rivaled Hollywood's productivity by the early 1930s, and newspapers and radio were well-established. Agriculture was declining in favor of industry, and heavy industry was especially subsidized. On the outskirts of Tokyo, people who had moved from the countryside to the city lived in large slums.

Before his departure, Father Lassalle had been inspired by a book written by a Protestant Japanese who lived and worked in the slums of the port city of Kobe. "If I were to go to Japan, my ideal would be to live in the slums," he said some fifty years later, toward the end of his life. His other intention was to learn about Zen, "because it is a typically Japanese thing. And because Zen has strongly influenced the character of the Japanese."[1]

First, however, the young priest became a "minister," or administrator, of the Jesuit mission in Tokyo. He was also in charge of Sophia University, which had just been approved by the Japanese government. With the money that his old university friend and fellow Jesuit Bruno Bitter had raised with great personal effort from abroad, the construction of the university began in 1931. Today, Sophia University is one of the leading universities in Japan.

The political and social situation in Japan was very tense. The rapid transition from a feudal society, where land and agriculture were the sources of wealth, to an industrial society left the peasants impoverished. In addition, the population was growing rapidly. Many Japanese fled poverty and hunger and immigrated to Latin America. In this situation, social work was necessary, and the Jesuits' motto was "social work as a means of apostolate." Efforts were made to strengthen the social awareness of the 1.4 percent of the Japanese people who were Catholic.

In the autumn of 1931, the Japanese army invaded Manchuria. In November of the same year, Father Hugo Lassalle founded a settlement in the slums of Tokyo, modeled on a similar project in London. This social service center still exists today. At that time, about 13 percent of Tokyo's population lived in the slum of Mikawashima. Together with two students, he moved from Sophia University to the social service center in the slums. The settlement offered food, medical care, a pharmacy, a school (also for adults), and legal advice. Father

---

[1] Hugo M. Enomiya-Lassalle, *Mein Weg zum Zen* (Kösel-Verlag, 2018), 20 (hereinafter MWZ).

Lassalle had also established a sociological research institute, which was a novelty in Japan at that time.

Social service is a form of care for "temporal things," as Father Lassalle put it.

Lassalle said that the "transcendent salvation" proclaimed by Christianity could not be imposed on people. Christmas celebrations, at which Hugo Lassalle played German songs (which were very popular in Japan) on his beloved cello, and summer camps for children were good opportunities to share the Gospel. During these events, Hugo Lassalle occasionally worked with Buddhist priests. He discussed religious questions with them, which led him to discover parallels between Buddhism and Christianity.[2] The settlement was proof that "great power, love, and selflessness reside in Christianity" and that *caritas*, "love," is a "pioneer of the Catholic faith,"[3] as Father Lassalle wrote. But no one would have let themselves be baptized for a handful of rice, he later said proudly.[4]

The situation of Christianity in Japan has never been easy. The Jesuits had brought Christianity to Japan in 1549. However, the Japanese shoguns, who had just taken power of the whole country at that time, soon became aware of the European powers' appetite for Japan. They closed Japan to the rest of the world, and Christianity was banned as a foreign religion. Those who did not officially renounce Christianity were executed. Only in the remotest parts of Japan did groups of Christians survive in secret, discovered by Catholic missionaries after Japan opened up.

This was in the second half of the nineteenth century. At that time, Japan was eagerly opening up to Western influences,

---

[2] *Aus dem Land der aufgehenden Sonne* no. 18 (September 1933): 240–41.

[3] MWZ, 40.

[4] Ursula Baatz, "Encounters: Western and Eastern Spirituality: Hugo M. Enomiya-Lassalle," Austrian Broadcasting Corporation (ORF), Ö1 – Radiokolleg, February 11–14, 1981.

and educated Japanese, in particular, discovered Christianity as the worldview of the superior foreign powers. But they quickly realized that the "long-nosed" were divided on religion—some were atheists and positivists, others Catholics or Protestants—and there was no platform for common ground. The rise of Japan as a major power in the Pacific region at the turn of the twentieth century and the strengthening of Japanese national sentiment caused Christianity to lose its appeal. In addition, the Japanese nation-state imposed a unified national religion. Shinto, the ancient village religion of Japan, became state Shinto. The *tenno* ("heavenly emperor") was revered as the descendant of the sun goddess Amaterasu, and her shrine at Ise was declared a national shrine.

Ancestor worship, an important social factor in East Asia, was also linked to the interests of the Japanese nation-state. The Yasukuni Shrine in Tokyo, dedicated to the fallen soldiers of the Russo-Japanese War, remains to this day a symbol of the unity of the Japanese nation. Paying respect to the spirits of the deceased at the Yasukuni Shrine was a civic duty. However, in 1932, two Catholic students at Sophia University refused to participate in this act of homage because they felt it was against the teachings of the catechism. The commanding officer in charge of military training at Sophia University reported the matter to the Minister of the Interior, and the Japanese newspapers stirred up hatred against Christians as traitors to the state.

The problem was that, according to Catholic canon law, a Catholic was at that time not allowed to participate in religious ceremonies of other religions. *Communicatio in sacris*, or "communication in the sacred," was prohibited. Negotiations between the Vatican and the Japanese Ministry of the Interior resulted in a compromise: Christians were allowed to participate in Shinto ceremonies, provided that the motive for participation was not religious in nature, but rather the fulfillment of civic, social, or family duties, and the Shinto ceremony was seen not as a religious act but as a custom. The good relationship between the Catholic Church and the Japanese state was restored, and at the same time, a small but significant step was taken. A precedent was set that could allow Catholics to participate in religious ceremonies of other religions under certain circumstances.

In March 1935, at the age of only thirty-seven, Father Lassalle was appointed superior of the German Jesuits in Japan by his former teacher, Wilhelm Klein, a charismatic and fiery character who died only in 1996 at the age of 107 in Münster, Westphalia. Father Lassalle was one of the few priests who spoke Japanese.[5] He believed that a missionary should not only know the language, culture, and customs of the country but should also adapt to the mentality as much as possible, that is, *become Japanese*.[6] The then-apostolic delegate for Japan, Paolo Marella, shared this view, which only gained widespread acceptance after the Second Vatican Council. But as early as 1919, Pope Benedict XV (1854–1922) had made it clear in the apostolic Letter *Maximum Illud* that mission was not to be equated with colonization; in mission countries the leadership should be taken over as soon as possible by priests of the respective country. Missionaries should also not introduce their own customs and traditions into the countries. The apostolic letter said that missions should serve the glory of God and the salvation of humanity.[7] In Jesuit circles, these ideas were further developed: adaptation, that is, accommodation to the

---

[5] Reported by P. Paul Pfister, SJ.

[6] *"Hausunterricht in Nagatsuka zur Gelübdeerneuerung"* ("Homeschooling in Nagatsuka to Renew Vows"), June 6, 1940 (unpublished manuscript).

[7] Benedict XV, *Maximum Illud*, no. 12 (1919). Quoted by Karl Müller, in *Missionstheologie. Eine Einführung* (Dietrich Reimer, 1985), 72.

country's culture, was the motto of Father Alfons Väth SJ, editor of the journal *Katholische Mission*. At a time, in the West, when anyone who was not Caucasian was considered a curiosity, the magazine argued that there were genuine qualities in other cultures.

In his new role as superior, Hugo Lassalle strongly advocated for a Japanese Christianity. The first Japanese-style Catholic church was built under his auspices near Hiroshima, at the Jesuit novitiate in Nagatsuka. He also advocated, albeit unsuccessfully, for the beatification of a seventeenth-century Christian samurai who died a martyr in Manila. And he wrote several times to Rome asking for permission to celebrate the Eucharist in Japanese instead of Latin. The request was denied; it was only after the Second Vatican Council that the use of the vernacular language for the liturgy was permitted.

The adaptation of the Catholic tradition to the Japanese culture and mentality was intended to help the people of Japan open themselves to *supernatural means*, to the intervention of divine grace. This was a vital interest for Hugo Lassalle. According to the beliefs of the time, anyone who was not baptized as a Roman Catholic could not find eternal bliss in heaven but would fall prey to eternal damnation—an unbearable thought for Hugo Lassalle. Therefore, he did his best to win people in Japan to Christianity. At the same time, the most important thing in the life of a missionary for Father Lassalle was his own spiritual path. This meant going through a personal process of transformation, renouncing ties to his homeland and heritage, and immersing himself in the new culture. Father Lassalle saw this as part of the spiritual path of a priest. The quest for union with God, the *unio mystica*, is the goal that he could not afford to overlook in all the necessary activities. Lassalle therefore organized his life accordingly, even if some found the consistency with which he did so rather harsh.

During his first years as superior, Father Lassalle was mainly involved in construction work. In 1936, the Jesuits had begun planning a novitiate in Nagatsuka, near the city of Hiroshima in southern Japan—today it is part of the city—and the following year they opened a high school in Rokko, near Osaka. The novitiate in Nagatsuka was in keeping with the missionary concept of accommodation: the rooms of the house were Japanese in style, with tatami mats, cupboards, and a tokonoma, an alcove with flowers and a calligraphy; the chapel was also based on Japanese ideas of sacred space. More than two thousand people attended the inauguration, and the effort to adapt to the Japanese way of life was generally well received, but not by Japanese Christians, who preferred a more European style. Nevertheless, the missionary program of "accommodation" sought "to penetrate deeper layers where the spirit of Christ must marry with the spirit of Japan, and this spirit of Japan has remained almost untouched by the Western influences that have so powerfully changed the face of Japan in recent decades,"[8] according to the young Jesuit Niklaus Luhmer.

However, the "Japanese spirit" at that time also had a political side, namely, a militarism and nationalism that eventually led to Japan's involvement in World War II. In 1936, the same year the Jesuits began building the novitiate in Nagatsuka, Hitler's Germany and Japan signed the Anti-Comintern Pact against Communist Russia, later joined by Franco's Spain and Mussolini's Italy. In China, the Red Army under Mao Zedong had allied against Japan with the Kuomintang Army under General Chiang Kai-shek. On July 3, 1937, there was a nighttime skirmish between Japanese and Chinese troops on the border of Japanese-occupied Manchuria, which Japan used as an excuse to invade Chinese territory. The victorious advance was celebrated in Tokyo with torchlight processions attended

---

[8] Niklaus Luhmer, "Ein Grundstein neuen Werdens: Noviziat in Hiroshima," in *Aus dem Land der aufgehenden Sonne*, no. 13 (1940), 140.

by millions of people,[9] marking the beginning of World War II in East Asia.

Japan considered itself responsible of securing Asia for Asians, and this was the justification for the invasion of China. A "Greater East Asian Economic Zone" under the leadership of Japan was to accomplish this.[10] National unity was considered essential for successful warfare. The *kokutai* ideology, familiar to the Japanese since the Meiji period, legitimized imperialist policy with a belief in the divinity of the emperor, the uniqueness of the Japanese people, and Japan's mission to bridge the gap between East and West. The enforced conformity of all aspects of public life was justified by the old virtues of loyalty, filial piety, and patriotism, along with state control of religion. There was little vocal opposition, for anyone who openly opposed the "Japanese mission to Asia" was thrown in jail. Even the Christians of Japan hardly raised their voices against this policy. They were afraid of reinforcing the existing prejudice that Christians behaved in an "un-Japanese" manner.

After a short trip to Rome in the fall of 1938 to attend the General Congregation of the Jesuits, Hugo Lassalle moved from Tokyo to Hiroshima in the spring of 1939. In addition to his duties as superior, he also served as pastor of the Hiroshima parish. Hiroshima has a Christian tradition dating back to the first missionary work of the Jesuits in the sixteenth century. Hiroshima was a city with a strong middle class, and there was a very active Catholic parish. In addition to catechism classes for those interested, Lassalle and his staff offered language courses, and Lassalle also taught French at the nearby naval base in Kure. The language classes were popular, as were the

---

[9] *Aus dem Land der aufgehenden Sonne*, no. 13.
[10] Janet E. Hunter, *The Emergence of Modern Japan: An Introductory History Since 1853* (Pearson Education, 1989).

musical evenings, for which Lassalle borrowed the shellac records from the owner of a local geisha house. Occasionally, he gave small concerts on the cello. However, the missionary work itself was not very successful. Although there were many who were interested in Christianity, those who converted and were baptized would have to existentially question their social relationships, and few were willing to take that risk.

Together with professors from Bunrika University in Hiroshima, including philosophy professor Taro Eto, Lassalle founded a Catholic study group in the winter of 1939. A group of thirty to forty people regularly studied books by German-speaking Catholic authors under Lassalle's guidance. Through his conversations with the professors, Hugo Lassalle gradually became interested in Zen and read books about it.[11]

After the Japanese occupation of Indochina, the US terminated its trade agreements. Japan's economy depended on the import of raw materials, especially oil and iron. The Japanese army and navy urged the emperor to declare war on the US. The bombing of Pearl Harbor was the beginning of the war with the US. Initially, Japanese troops were victorious and occupied the Philippines, Singapore, Burma (now Myanmar), and the Dutch East Indies (now Indonesia). The brutality of the Japanese occupation is still fresh in the memories of the people of these countries. In April 1942, the US Army halted the Japanese advance; a year later, in February 1943, the German army surrendered at Stalingrad; and in September of the following year, Mussolini's troops surrendered. Little of this trickled down to Japan, where the media maintained a triumphalist narrative. However, basic foodstuffs, coal, firewood, oil, and clothing became scarce and were rationed.

Amid the war, in the winter of 1943, Hugo Lassalle decided

---

[11] MWZ, 43.

to follow the advice of his acquaintances and not only read books on Zen but also attend a sesshin.

In February 1943, Lassalle attended his first sesshin at the Temple of Eternal Light, a Soto Zen temple in Tsuwano, near Hiroshima. He later recalled, "By the way, I was prepared for the worst. Apart from the uncomfortable way of sitting, I had heard and read a lot about the strictness of these Zen monasteries. . . . So I was all the more surprised when, on the day of my arrival, a big banquet was prepared for me, with rice wine and many typical delicacies, which I enjoyed together with the bonzes."[12] Sesshin literally means "gathering of the heart." The day begins with *zazen* ("sitting in absorption") early in the morning, usually long before sunrise. This is followed by sutra recitation and a meager breakfast of rice gruel. Work such as housecleaning, gardening, or kitchen duties are also part of the daily routine, which consists essentially of many periods of zazen, interspersed with shorter periods of walking. The sesshin usually includes ten or more hours of "sitting."

The February sesshin in Tsuwano was cold and wintry because Zen temples have no furnaces. Father Lassalle was given three "hibachi," or fire basins, which he placed in his room. But there was no remedy for the pain in his legs that soon began. "Now I know what purgatory is," he told Father Cieslik, his chaplain, when he returned.[13] The rigorous practice made a deep and lasting impression, and Lassalle had little trouble seeing the parallels between Zen Buddhist asceticism and Jesuit asceticism.

The political situation continued to escalate. While the Japanese troops were increasingly forced onto the defensive, the pressure on the conformist population in Japan itself increased.

---

[12] MWZ, 46.
[13] Reported by Fr. Hubert Cieslik.

Under the pretext of wanting to be baptized, police informers infiltrated the parish. As a result, Father Pedro Arrupe, who later became Superior General of the Jesuits, and some Japanese Christians were imprisoned for a time on suspicion of espionage. Hugo Lassalle burned his diaries at the time, fearing that the Japanese underground police might find the names of Japanese Christians and then persecute them. As a German citizen, Lassalle was considered an ally of Japan, which saved him from internment, but his rights were restricted. When Lassalle once asked the Japanese police for permission to travel for a visitation, he was told to come back in a month.[14] After a month, he was told to come back in three weeks, and after that, he was put off again, and so on. This was the Japanese way of telling him that his request had been rejected. But Lassalle persisted. When, after many fruitless attempts, he was summoned to the police station at midnight, he arrived promptly at midnight. He was finally granted permission to travel.

In November 1944, the Americans began to bomb Japanese cities extensively, in some cases using incendiary bombs. American troops landed on Okinawa in April 1945. Kamikaze pilots were able to delay the American advance, but with Germany's surrender, Japan had run out of options. There were informal contacts between Japan and the Allies, and at the Potsdam Conference in July 1945, the victorious powers demanded the total surrender of Japan. But this was met with little approval from Japanese leadership circles.

Hiroshima was spared from bombing until August 1945. Despite the war, Lassalle organized a weekly record concert—a form of recreation for the participants. The morning of August 6 began like any other. Breakfast consisted of bread made from beans, which caused stomach pains and nothing

---

[14] Reported by P. Paul Pfister.

else. The morning air alarm went off as usual after breakfast and passed without incident. Father Lassalle was in his office. It was a quarter past eight. A single plane appeared over the city. No alarm sounded. Suddenly, a bright light flashed.

"Then everything collapsed above me. It went completely dark, everything was full of dust, and I thought that this would be the end of me." The next thought was, "Now I will know what heaven is really like."[15] "Gradually, the dust settled and light came back into the room. The windows and walls were shattered. I hadn't fallen over, but I thought I would soon be dead,"[16] Lassalle said decades later. There is no detailed personal account from him of that day. The following summary of the events in Hiroshima on August 6, 1945, comes from Father Siemes.[17]

> *The church, the catechist's house, and all the houses around it immediately collapsed. Although seriously wounded in the back and leg and bleeding profusely, Father Lassalle helped to free people who were screaming for help under the rubble. A wall of fire was approaching. They gathered a few things from the presbytery, buried them in the square in front of the church, and fled from the approaching wall of fire. Fukai, the secretary of the mission administration, did not want to go with them. He is unharmed but declares that he will not survive the destruction of his homeland. The fathers drag him away by force. People buried under the rubble of their houses scream for help from the approaching fire.*

---

[15] Helmut E. Lück, *Atomic Bomb and Meditation? Portrait of the Jesuit and Zen Master Hugo M. Enomiya-Lassalle*, NDR Television, February 23, 1985.
[16] MWZ, 64.
[17] See also https://nsarchive.gwu.edu/document/30506-document-25-atomic-bomb-hiroshima-eyewitness-account-p-siemes-nd-translated-germa.

Father Siemes writes:

They must be left to their fate. The place outside the city where people are trying to flee is no longer accessible. They make their way to Asano Park. Fukai does not want to continue and stays behind. Nothing more is heard of him. In the park, people flee to the riverbank. Since the raging fire had spread, a strong wind was blowing. Around two in the afternoon, it became a hurricane. It was getting dark. A cyclone came raging down the river from the sea. Father Kleinsorge threw himself over Father Schiffer to protect him. The others clung to the floor. The housekeeper, standing upright, is swept into the river. Heavy uprooted trees fly over her, and the river's water is driven up several feet. . . . A little further downstream, at the bridge where the refugees have gathered, many are swept into the river. The park is filled with refugees. Most are injured and have lost loved ones they had to leave behind under the collapsing buildings or lost sight of as they fled. There is no help for the wounded. Some are dying. No one cares if there is a dead body next to them. . . .

It is difficult to transport our wounded. They cannot be adequately bandaged in the dark. During the transport over the fallen trees in the park, they are shaken so much that they lose life-threatening amounts of blood. The guardian angel in this situation is a Protestant pastor we know. He has found a boat and is willing to take our wounded downriver to a place where we can get along more easily.

First, Father Schiffer and two other priests went downriver. *"When the boat returned after half an hour, the priest called for help to rescue two children he had found floating upstream. The children were pulled from the river. They had burns. Soon they began to shiver and died in the park.*

Lassalle was loaded into the boat with a priest and a theology student. Father Cieslik feels strong enough to walk to Nagatsuka, and Father Kleinsorge, who cannot walk that far, stays behind in the park with the housekeeper and will be picked up the next day.

From across the river, the piercing neighing of horses threatened by the fire echoes through the night. We land on a sandbar connected to the shore. It is full of wounded people who have escaped the fire by fleeing into the river. They scream for help, begging us to save them, afraid of drowning when the river rises from the sea with the tide and submerges the sandbar. They are too weak to move themselves.

But the small group must continue.

The wounded cry for water. We help some of them. Out of the darkness, we hear cries for help, but we cannot reach

*them because of the rubble. A group of soldiers comes
along. When the officer notices that we are speaking a
foreign language, he immediately draws his sword, shouts
at us who we are, and wants to strike us.*

He mistakes the priests for American paratroopers. They
manage to calm him down, and he lets them go.

Lassalle begins to feel the effects of his injuries and loss of
blood. He is cold despite the heat. He is carried on a stretcher
to the outskirts of the city. The city is largely burnt out, writes
Father Siemes.

*Only sometimes do we hear cries for help as we pass by.
The strange smell of smoke that stings our nostrils is that of
burnt corpses. The figure sitting upright in the rubble that
we saw on the way is still there. It must have been very painful for Father Superior to be transported on a stretcher tied
together with planks. His entire back is covered with broken
glass. On a narrow road outside the city, a car approaches
and forces us to the side of the road. The porters on the left
fall with the stretcher into a six-foot-deep ditch, which we
did not see in the darkness. Father Superior disguises his
pain with a dry joke. But with the stretcher that no longer
holds together, it is impossible to go on like this.*

Lassalle was transferred to a handcart, and finally, at four
o'clock in the morning, twenty hours after the atomic bombing, they arrived in Nagatsuka.

*Where the city used to be, as far as the eye can see, is
a desert of ash and debris. Only a few concrete buildings remain, their interiors completely destroyed by fire.
The banks of the river are littered with corpses and the
wounded. The rising water has already submerged bod-
ies here and there. Along the main road in the district*

of Hakushima, the naked, burnt corpses are piled up particularly densely. Among them are the wounded who are still alive. They lay exposed to the hot sun. Some have crawled under burned-out cars and streetcars. Horribly mutilated figures stagger towards us and then collapse before our eyes.

The fathers take with them those they can transport. In the hospital, the wounded lay in the devastated corridors, abandoned and dying. The presbytery was reduced to ashes, with pieces of melted metal from the sacred vessels. Fifty refugees are housed in Nagatsuka and are being cared for as best as possible by Father Pedro Arrupe, who is also a doctor.

Our work in those days gave more prestige to Christianity than all our work in the many years before. . . . In the following days, funeral processions passed by our house from morning to night. The dead were taken to a remote valley for cremation. People carried bundles of wood and personally cremated their family members. Late at night, the valley was still lit by the firelight of the pyres.

Two hundred thousand people died immediately as a result of the first atomic bomb, and many more would slowly succumb to its effects over the following decades. Even today, the Hiroshima hospitals are at full capacity treating victims of the atomic bomb. The current occupants of the hospital were children on August 6, 1945.

On August 9, the Americans dropped another atomic bomb on Nagasaki. The army continued to protest against a ceasefire. On August 15, Emperor Hirohito announced Japan's surrender over the radio. The ceasefire was signed on December 2 aboard the American flagship Missouri in Tokyo Bay.

This marked the end of World War II. A new era dawned for Japan.

4

The Peace Memorial Church

❧

When Father Hugo Lassalle had recovered somewhat from his injuries, he and Father Cieslik moved into a small corrugated iron hut on the site of the presbytery. Hiroshima was completely destroyed, as were most of the other major cities in Japan, which were practically burned to the ground by the American attacks. Nearly one million civilians died in the bombings. One-third of the Japanese population was homeless, but there were no building materials and, most importantly, nothing to eat. The US occupying power brought new and unfamiliar foods to Japan—tons of flour, corn, and powdered milk, but also chocolate and chewing gum. In addition, the political changes skillfully implemented by General MacArthur, the supreme commander of US forces in Japan, had an even greater impact on the Japanese way of life. The new constitution, which went into effect in January 1946, lowered the voting age to twenty and gave women the right to vote for the first time.

The supreme command of the American occupation forces abolished compulsory religious, ethical, and political education in schools. This was done primarily to stop the spread of

Japanese nationalist ideology. The emperor was no longer to be seen as an absolute, divine monarch, as the descendant of the sun goddess Amaterasu, and as the embodiment of the nation-state. The leading figures of the defeated Japanese nation-state were stripped of their power: politicians and generals directly responsible for the war were tried as war criminals, senior officials who also bore responsibility were forced to resign, and high-ranking Buddhist monks and priests were also affected by this measure. The "thought police" was abolished, political prisoners were released from jail, independent trade unions were established, and the Communist Party was allowed to reform. Religious freedom was also established. In November 1945, Emperor Hirohito ritually announced Japan's defeat as "Descendant of the Sun" to the sun goddess Amaterasu at the national shrine in Ise. And in January 1946, Hirohito read a decree on Japanese radio in his own voice, declaring that he was not of divine descent.

The belief in the invincibility of Japan and the divine origin of the Japanese nation was shaken, for the gods of Japan had failed. The emotional and spiritual vacuum of the postwar period almost exceeded the material hardship, wrote Father Bruno Bitter, Lassalle's old friend and rector of Sophia University at the time.

In the years immediately after the war, there was an enormous interest in Christianity. Hugo Lassalle's plans to create a Japanese Christianity seemed destined to be fulfilled. He shared Bruno Bitter's assessment, as he wrote in a letter to a US captain: "Anyone who wants to can now become a Christian [. . .] It was certainly more than a coincidence that this change took place exactly on the anniversary of the arrival of Francis Xavier, the first Christian missionary in Japan."[1]

Lectures on Christianity were in great demand, and even

---

[1] Letter to U.S. Captain Eastman, June 2, 1946 (unpublished).

the Japanese imperial family considered converting to Christianity, which was prevented by General MacArthur, as secret papers prove.[2]

The aim of MacArthur was to reduce not only the influence of state Shinto but also that of the Buddhist monasteries, which had traditionally been centers of power in Japan. This was done, for example, by redistributing the land of the monasteries, turning the tenants of monastic land into independent landowners. There was also an attempt essentially to dissolve the informal neighborhood associations that provided financial support to the temples. At the same time, there was a general climate of change in Japanese public life, and the profound transformation of society met with surprisingly little resistance. MacArthur was very sympathetic to Japan and its people, and the Japanese saw in him a great man of their own liking. Moreover, General MacArthur believed that democracy, "as we interpret it," was the realization of Christian principles and that Japan's spiritual void needed to be filled to prevent the advance of communism.[3] Therefore, he supported the efforts of Protestants and Catholics to Christianize Japan. When a pilgrimage was to take place in 1949 to commemorate the four hundredth anniversary of the landing of St. Francis Xavier, Bruno Bitter, then rector of Sophia University, asked the general for permission. "This is just what Japan needs now," General MacArthur replied, and the pilgrimage was approved.[4] It began in Nagasaki and went to all the cities that Francis Xavier had visited, including Osaka and Tokyo. Two relics were brought from Spain: the cross with which Francis Xavier had blessed people four hundred years earlier, together with his right upper arm, which had been taken

---

[2] William Woodard, *The Allied Occupation of Japan 1945–1952 and Japanese Religions* (Brill, 1972). See the documents in Appendix G, 351–59.

[3] Woodard, *The Allied Occupation of Japan 1945–1952.* See the documents in Appendix G, 351–59.

[4] Bruno Bitter, autobiography, 1971, unpublished manuscript, 47.

from his body, which is otherwise buried in Goa, and had been transferred to Europe.

The relics inspired the Japanese, and the newspapers wrote that Francis Xavier had come back to Japan after the lost war to bless the Japanese people. Prince Takamatsu, representing the emperor, spoke of a second coming of Francis Xavier to Japan. "It was now time to honor the high ideals of the Gospel." Such words from a member of the imperial family, commented Father Bitter in his memoir, would have been unthinkable thirty years later, in the 1970s.[5]

In August 1946, Lassalle left Yokohama for Europe via San Francisco. The General Congregation of the Jesuits took place in Rome, but the large meeting of Jesuit superiors was only one goal of the trip. Another was to collect money for the construction of a Peace Memorial Church in Hiroshima, and he also wanted to recruit staff for the Japanese mission.

During his visits with Cardinals Spellman (New York) and Cushing (Boston), Lassalle tried not only to raise money for the Peace Memorial Church but also to convey an understanding of the Japanese situation. He did this wherever he stayed for any length of time on this trip.

From Boston he flew to Rome, and after the conclusion of the General Congregation, he traveled through devastated postwar Germany. He probably took the opportunity to visit his mother and his two sisters, Elisabeth and Maria, who all still lived in Hildesheim. Contact with them through letters had been completely interrupted by the war. Lassalle maintained contact with the rest of his family—his younger brother Hans, who was disabled, had already died in 1930, and their father Georg Lassalle in 1940—until the death of his sisters. Maria died in 1978, and Lisbeth in 1985, five years before Lassalle's death.

---

[5] Bitter, autobiography 52.

Hildesheim, the city where Hugo Lassalle had spent his childhood, was bombed shortly before the end of the war, and most of the old churches in the town lay in ruins. The situation was similar to that of other German cities that Lassalle had visited. His brief notes on life in postwar Germany, on hunger, crop failures, the relationship of the population to the occupying powers, and the problems of denazification show him to be a keen observer. The change in people's thinking particularly struck him: they were interested in religion and liked to come to his lectures, *but they had forgotten how to think and were much more difficult to influence than people 25–35 years earlier.*[6] He realized that the religious language and the usual rhetoric of presenting Christian spirituality no longer resonated with people. It seems that the first signs of what Hugo Lassalle later diagnosed as the emerging "new consciousness" were already appearing.

A young nun from the Carmelite convent in Berlin was present at one of Lassalle's lectures on Japan and the atomic bomb,[7] and she still remembers the encounter vividly. Father Lassalle spoke very matter-of-factly and was by no means terribly pious, and he also told of his rescue without pathos. However, she remembers that he spoke with great emotion about the people of Hiroshima. At the time, the sixteen-year-old wanted to go to Japan as a missionary, so she went to talk to him. She was fascinated by his face, which seemed very Japanese to her. But what impressed her most was the way Lassalle listened to her. He took her seriously, and she felt as if she had grown a few centimeters in those moments. He promised to look for a suitable order for her. And a few weeks later, in fact, a postcard arrived with the address of a religious house.

Lassalle traveled via Switzerland back to Rome, where he

---

[6] 1946, undated, most likely after November 16.
[7] Interview with Sister Maria-Theresia, OCarm (OCD).

tried again to get Japanese recognized as a liturgical language in Japan—again in vain. At the beginning of January, he was in Spain. He lectured everywhere about the atomic bomb, the planned construction of the Peace Memorial Church, and the importance of the mission in Japan. Sometimes surprising sources of money opened up: for example, when students gave him the money for the tabernacle of the new church—the result of intensive stamp collecting. Along the way, Father Lassalle passed his driving test in Madrid. Two days later, on February 22, 1947, the Spanish dictator, Generalissimo Franco, received him in an audience that lasted more than an hour. Lassalle found the caudillo very cordial and fundamentally Catholic. He wrote down only parts of the conversation and only those passages that dealt with the need for social justice and how to overcome communism. But he probably also talked to Franco about the Japanese mission.

The following destinations were Argentina and Brazil. In view of the long-distance flight across the Atlantic, Lassalle had some anxious thoughts—no wonder, as long-distance flights were no walk in the park at that time. The planes that crossed the Atlantic were converted bombers and military transport planes, four-engine propeller aircraft, and the conditions for the twenty to a maximum of thirty-six passengers were anything but comfortable.

On March 7, 1947, just one day after arriving in Buenos Aires, Lassalle began a series of lectures that took him to the country's major cities. Argentina's authoritarian leader Juan Perón had only been in power for a year, and the social and political tensions in the country were very tangible to the traveler. The political alliance between large sections of the Catholic clergy and the Peronist regime had a negative impact on Lassalle's project. The propertied class, which was opposed to Peron was also opposed to the Catholic Church. Lassalle noticed that *although the country was very wealthy and the income was high, people gave little at the lectures*. In contrast to the Catholics, the few Protestant Argentines were more generous. But this did not change Lassalle's fundamental distrust of Protestants, who at the time seemed as suspect as Communists. The Second Vatican Council and its spirit of reconciliation were still a long way off.

Lassalle also used his four months in Argentina to publish his book on the atomic bomb and its consequences in Spanish. It was a plea for Japan and its culture and for peace in the world. An English edition had been blocked in Japan by the American occupation forces.

The next stop on his journey was Brazil, which, like Argentina, was a prosperous country at the time and a destination for many emigrants from Europe. As in Argentina, Lassalle gave lectures to Japanese immigrants in order to tell them as an eyewitness about the defeat of Japan and the surrender, which was unbelievable for them. Two thousand people attended his first lecture in São Paulo. Only a minority of the Japanese living in Brazil accepted the news of Japan's defeat, while the majority continued to believe in the emperor's victory. There were rumors that the tenno would proclaim himself emperor of the world and that a Japanese air force would land in Brazil. Evil profiteers set up shipping lines and other bogus companies to sell their fellow countrymen land—and tickets to it—somewhere in the supposedly newly conquered Japanese territories. There were also armed groups who, in the name of the "victors," murdered the "traitors" who claimed that Japan had lost. Even the Japanese newspapers in Brazil kept a low profile; as a result, especially those Japanese who lived in the interior of the country, peasants who did not speak Portuguese, firmly believed in Japan's victory. This belief, as Lassalle noted in a report he wrote on his return to Boston, was the result of nationalist education. There were massive attempts to disrupt the overall thirty-five lectures during the one-and-a-half months in Brazil, and Lassalle's Japanese hosts occasionally feared for his life. But that did not stop him from lecturing.

On August 29, Lassalle traveled via Rio de Janeiro to New York, once again crossing the entire North American continent, always on his missionary way. Since he had to wait a month for his passport to be cleared in Tokyo before leaving San Francisco, he used the time for his annual retreat. It was then that he first felt the desire to travel as a kind of itinerant preacher, like the mystics of the Middle Ages, *speaking about the One thing they did = the path to mystical union with God.*[8]

But it would be more than twenty years before this desire was realized.

By the end of November, Lassalle was back in Japan, but he did not get a moment's rest. He traveled more than a thousand kilometers between Tokyo and Yamaguchi in Kyushu in southern Japan to visit Jesuit institutions. He sought support for the Japanese in Brazil and made another attempt to obtain Japanese citizenship. He had first tried this in the early 1940s but was unsuccessful. This time he succeeded, and the German Jesuit Hugo Lassalle took a new name as a Japanese citizen: Enomiya Makibi, a name that linked him to Hiroshima and Japanese culture. Enomiya is the name of a Shinto shrine in Hiroshima, built on the spot where Jimmu Tenno, the legendary emperor of ancient times, is said to have landed in Japan. Kibi no Makibi was a scholar who lived in the eighth century; he was sent to China to study and returned more than twenty years later with books, weapons, musical instruments, and Buddhist images and writings, thus promoting Japan's cultural development.[9]

By the fall of 1948, much had been rebuilt. Public life had been transformed by new laws enacted by the American occupation forces and negotiated with the Japanese government. The large, financially powerful conglomerates, the *zaibatsu*,

---

[8] October 31, 1947.
[9] Kitamura Bunji, Kibi no Makibi, *Kodansha Encyclopedia of Japan*, vol. 5 (Kodansha USA, 1983), 201.

which had virtually dominated prewar politics, had been dissolved. In its new constitution, Japan explicitly renounced the right to wage war, including the right to have armed troops. New textbooks were introduced that emphasized the importance of the individual. The mythological–political worldview of state Shinto, which aimed to create a unified Japanese people, was banned, and the emperor was disempowered as the representative of this political order.

The old Prussian model of a class-based electoral system, introduced in Japan in the nineteenth century, had been replaced by an American-style representative democracy. All citizens, including women, were eligible to vote, as men and women had been granted equal rights under the constitution in 1947. Women were now allowed to walk alongside men in public, not just behind them as before.[10] A photograph by the famous Japanese photographer Kimura Ihei shows a Japanese couple crossing the street. Both are wearing Western clothes and walking side by side at the same speed. To European eyes, the photo is entirely unspectacular, but it symbolized the end of an era. Before the war, such a couple would have been prosecuted by the police for indecent behavior.

American films, but also the behavior of some American occupation soldiers, intensified the collision between new Western values and traditional Japanese culture. Above all, this mainly affected the way the sexes interacted.

Lassalle summarized his impressions in a lecture he gave in Yamaguchi in October 1949. Immediately after the war, there had been an increase in theft and robbery, but *as far as morality in the strict sense was concerned, people were still living according to the old ways. The attitude of Japanese women*

---

[10] *Cf.* Shunsuke Tsurumi, *A Cultural History of Postwar Japan, 1945–1980* (Routledge, 1987), chaps. 1 and 2; John W. Hall, *Das Japanische Kaiserreich,* (Fischer Taschenbuch 1968), chap. 20; J. Robert, "Japan und Korea seit 1945," in *Das moderne Asien,* ed. Lucien Bianco (Fischer Bucherei, 1969), 251–84.

toward the occupation was exemplary, perhaps better than in other countries. With democracy, however, social freedom was also introduced: a freedom that was particularly evident in the libertarian behavior of young Japanese men and women.

According to Lassalle, however, the real problem was much more complex. After the defeat of the nation, its ideals were shattered. *Democracy is all well and good in theory but not so easy to implement in practice, especially in countries like Japan, where people are used to collectivism.* There is nihilism among the educated classes in Japan, and those who are practically minded live according to materialistic and capitalistic principles: *that is, they look out only for themselves. These are all different forms of despair, of spiritual suicide. They no longer have any ideals.*[11]

In view of this situation, Lassalle said, the preservation of Japan's ideals, spirituality, and culture was of primary importance, and the Christianization of the Japanese people was of secondary importance. However, such thoughts were not heard until almost two decades later after the Second Vatican Council. At the end of the 1940s, Lassalle met with little approval from his colleagues, which often depressed him. *I am utterly unsuitable for the office of superior at this time because my thoughts are so different from those of the other priests. This constraint is unbearable for me. I have to provide leadership in a position of authority, following guidelines with responsibility that go against my beliefs.*[12] However, he tried to do this to the best of his conscience, even if he sometimes treated his subordinates too harshly, as he thought.

The daily concerns of a pastor and missionary took up most of his time: difficulties with the parents of a candidate for baptism, problems with mixed marriages, or the procurement and

---

[11] "Das Christentum und die Probleme der Gegenwart," Yamaguchi, October 19, 1948, 5 (unpublished manuscript).
[12] June 29, 1948.

administration of forms, incense, prayer, hymn books, and catechisms. In addition, Lassalle was the superior of several building projects: the destroyed Ignatius Church in Tokyo was rebuilt, and in Hiroshima the long-planned Elisabeth Music University and an orphanage were built. Together with the Jesuit priests of the Hiroshima district, he prepared for 1948 a major speaking campaign similar to the one he had undertaken immediately after the war in 1946. At that time, the focus was on the new situation in Japan, democracy, Christianity, inflation, Japan's place in the world, the labor question, but also moral issues and questions about the meaning of life. The lecture tour took him all over Hiroshima Province. He spoke in a rubber factory, to police officers, in Buddhist temples, and at various craftsmen's guilds, sometimes to small audiences and sometimes to crowds of hundreds, about his trip around the world, about Germany after the war, and about the problems of modernization in Japan.

The biggest project of these years, however, was the planning and construction of the Peace Memorial Church in Hiroshima. The call for tenders was issued together with Japan's largest and most prestigious daily newspaper, the *Asahi Shimbun*. It called for a church building that would be *modern, monumental, religious, and Japanese*.[13] However, none of the submissions met all of these criteria. In the end, the renowned architect Murano Togo (1891–1984) was commissioned to build the church. In his design, he emphasized the characteristic features of Zen art: asymmetry, simplicity, naturalness, and "noble austerity."[14] These can be seen in the details of the large, very sober concrete structure of the Peace Memorial Church. The irregularly protruding brown bricks of the exterior walls create patterns of shadows that change throughout the day with

---

[13] June 29, 1948 and Hugo M. Enomiya-Lassalle, *Mein Weg zum Zen* (Kösel-Verlag, 2018), 71 (hereinafter MWZ).

[14] *Cf.* Shin'ich Hisamatsu, *Zen and the Fine Arts* (Kodansha International, 1971), 28ff.

the position of the sun. Over the decades, tiny mosses and lichens have settled on the unglazed and unplastered surface of the bricks. Like a Shinto temple, there is a water basin in front of the church's portal, with a bridge leading across it. This symbolism was used in the first Christian churches in Japan in the sixteenth century. "The path from the profane to the religious crosses a bridge, and the crossing of the water becomes a symbol of purification before entering the sacred precinct,"[15] Lassalle explained the symbolism in later years.

The real and lasting problem with the church building, however, was money: the sum that Lassalle had collected on his trip through Europe and South and North America was nowhere near enough. He therefore launched a major fundraising campaign with a committee headed by Prince Takamatsu and Prime Minister Yoshida. However, the construction cost was far more than expected. Hiroshima is located by the sea and was built on the alluvial sands of a river delta. During the excavation of the foundations, it became clear that the plans would have to be changed to prevent the church from being flooded at high tide. To raise the necessary funds, Lassalle went begging to large companies and influential people in Tokyo, sometimes several times a week. These trips were very humiliating for him, as he was often rejected. In a diary entry dated December 28, 1951, he noted that he had traveled back and forth between Hiroshima and Tokyo twenty-seven times that year; that's a total of about 44,000 kilometers by train, mostly on night trains and standing up. During these years, he learned to sleep standing up, according to his Jesuit colleague Father Cieslik.

He once complained in a letter that he was *a railroad yard for money*.[16] A large donation from the US relieved him for a short time, but then he lost heart, fearing that he would be unable to complete the project on his own. Another time, he

---

[15] MWZ, 72.
[16] Letter to Fr. Wilhelm Schiffer, SJ, 1951 (unpublished).

faithfully lent a large sum of money to someone for the production of a movie. The person in question was unable to repay the money, and Lassalle and his Japanese friends considered whether the money could be recovered by staging bullfights, which would have been a sensation in Japan at the time. In the end, Lassalle's friend Father Bruno Bitter, who was in charge of the Jesuits' finances, came to the rescue and provided the money needed to complete the church.

Although Lassalle had not been the superior of the Jesuits since March 1949—Father Pfister had taken over as provincial for the newly founded, independent Japanese province— he had become vicar general of the diocese of Hiroshima and was thus responsible for almost all administrative matters. So he was caught between collecting funds, supervising construction, parish work, and his work as vicar general. The latter consisted mainly of office work, which he did not particularly like because it never ended and there were always new papers on the table. In this situation, he sought a new form of exercise and prayer to maintain his inner balance. He remembered the Zen practice he had learned during his first sesshin in the winter of 1943 and tried to incorporate the practice of silence into his daily prayer practice. During this time, he also discovered the power of silence: outer silence when facing criticism (not to justify, but to remain silent), and inner silence to maintain concentration and alignment with God. *The inner life should be the true vocation.*[17]

Lassalle's contact with Buddhist monks had intensified in recent years, especially after the founding of the Association for the Promotion of Religious Thought, *Shukyoshisokoyokai*, in August 1949. This association was initiated by a Soto-shu monk named Rurei Tojo. He had come to Sophia University and asked for lectures by the Fathers on the Catholic Church's position on communism. The background was the heighten-

---

[17] November 4, 1950.

ing of tensions of the Cold War. Since 1949, not only the US but also the Soviet Union had been in possession of nuclear weapons. Japan appeared to be an important strategic base for the Americans. There was talk of rearming Japan and creating a capitalist economic system in Japan based on the American model. The large corporations, the *zaibatsu*, which had been dissolved after the war, were reactivated, and work and consumption became important values. This gradually led to the disintegration of the traditional way of life with its strong social ties.

The association, as Lassalle later said, was to serve "cooperation for the understanding of religions in general and for the raising of the morals of the people, which are threatened by the ever-increasing materialism and communism."[18] Such cooperation between Christians and Buddhists against atheism and materialism had already been discussed in Japan at the end of the nineteenth century. In the late fall of 1949, Lassalle and the Zen monk Tojo began a series of lectures in various Zen temples in the Hiroshima area. The two traveled in an old jeep to remote areas high in the mountains, where farmers still lived in the traditional way. They spent the nights in temples that, like all traditional houses in Japan, have no glass windows and instead have sliding doors with rice paper stuck on them as windows. In late fall and winter, it gets bitterly cold even in southern Japan, so the nights in the temple would have been freezing.

This collaboration with the Soto-shu Zen temples, one of the two major Zen traditions firmly established in Japan (the other being Rinzai-shu), remained one of Father Lassalle's main activities until the 1960s. His interest in Zen grew, and in the spring of 1952, he visited the main temple of Soto-shu, Eiheiji, which the great Zen master Dogen had founded in the thir-

---

[18] MWZ, 48. Compare for this section MWZ, 47–50.

teenth century in a remote area of western Japan. In June, he traveled to Tsurumi with Father Heinrich Dumoulin, who later became an expert on Zen Buddhism, another priest, and his old friend, the philosophy professor Taro Eto, who had introduced Lassalle to Zen and had himself been baptized by Lassalle and become a Christian. This suburb of the large port city of Yokohama is home to the Sojiji, the second main temple of Soto-shu, and the abbot of the Sojiji, Genshu Watanabe (1869–1963), was one of the most important Zen masters of his time. The questions the priests asked him about Zen were answered by the roshi in his own way, for example, "*Past, present, future, all is death.*"[19] Although Lassalle could not understand the meaning of these statements at the time, this encounter set an important course for Hugo Lassalle's later life.

Fr. Enomiya-Lassalle and Professor Taro Eto from Bunrika University, Hiroshima, and his wife. It was Professor Taro Eto who brought Lassalle to Zen. (Probably taken in early 1980s).

[19] July 22, 1952.

Lassalle's relationship with the Zen priests was very intense, and when he called them "bonze," it was not meant pejoratively but was merely a common term at the time. Some of the Zen priests even helped him raise money for the church building. "The extent of our success is also shown by the suggestion of some Buddhist leaders that we select suitable monks to serve as 'catechists' to promote the Catholic religion. This may seem paradoxical, and indeed it is, but it shows the goodwill of these Buddhist leaders," writes Lassalle. These extraordinary developments were reported to Rome, where it was pointed out that Buddhist priests were willing to work as Christian catechists, but no interest was expressed on the Christian side.

The construction of the church gradually came to an end. In February 1953, the four bells, financed by donations from Bochum (Germany), were hung in the tower. The names of the bells were programmatic: one was dedicated to Mary, Queen of Peace; one to Francis Xavier, the Apostle of Japan; one to Peter Canisius, the Apostle of Germany (like Francis Xavier, one of the original Jesuits); and the fourth was named after the Japanese Jesuit martyr Paul Miki (1564–1597).

Nine years after the atomic bombing of Hiroshima, the Peace Memorial Church was inaugurated on August 6, 1954. The interior was financed mainly by German donations. The main altar, made of black marble and donated by Belgian Catholics, arrived at the port of Yokohama on August 5 and was transported to Hiroshima, arriving at midnight on a special freight car on the only express train that ran between Tokyo and Hiroshima at that time. The altar was installed that evening, and the ceremony began on time. Prince Takamatsu, the highest-ranking admiral of the Japanese fleet, ambassadors from various European countries, politicians, and various superiors of religious orders were present. It was a grand celebration that deeply moved Hugo Lassalle, so much so that he felt a special consolation on this day of the inauguration of the church that he had initiated and whose construction he had supervised.

After the inauguration, at the end of the day, Monsignor Ogihara, the Apostolic Administrator of Hiroshima, in agreement with the Jesuit Provincial, informed Father Lassalle that he would not be the pastor of the Peace Memorial Church.

5

On the Way of Zen

❧

The construction of the Peace Memorial Church was essentially completed, another Jesuit had taken over the parish, and Lassalle was assigned to a newly created position for missionary affairs, but its establishment was delayed. His removal from the parish deeply saddened him. He was now fifty-seven years old, and although he had no material worries as a member of the order, he lacked a perspective for the remaining years of his life. In this situation, he felt that the most appropriate thing to do was to seek inner peace and freedom. So he retired to the novitiate in Nagatsuka for a four-week spiritual retreat, *a new beginning for the last stage of my life.*[1] The longing for God became more and more the motive of his life, and he decided *to continue to long for union with God, to continue to strive for it,*[2] which meant a constant effort to "peel off," to disidentify, to become less and less self-centered in everyday things. It also meant, in the discursive prayer of the "Two Standards" in the Spiritual Exercises of Ignatius, to decide again and more deeply

---

[1] January 16, 1955.
[2] February 3, 1955.

for *poverty as a way to holiness*, and thus not to be attached to anything. *Only when this is achieved will the day of freedom dawn. Only then can I be truly happy.*[3] The "third degree of humility," *the madness of the saints*, should be the basis for this final stage of life. *The third degree of humility, however, does not mean just loving God, but perhaps being in love with God, where reason is no longer dominant but only love. All the saints must have had this degree.*[4] All emotional and self-centered criteria, even "consolations," the positive feelings given while praying, were to be abandoned. He wanted to try to see everything in the light of God, *with all the light of reason and grace at my disposal. So more quiet reflection than the flow of impulses, although intuition does not have to be turned off.*"[5]

After the retreat, he spent another three weeks in a sanatorium. Apparently, his health had deteriorated. Perhaps the pulmonary tuberculosis that had existed before the war had returned. He then returned to the parish in Noboricho, Hiroshima. He tried to see his situation—the constant failure of his plans for a form of mission that would integrate Christianity into Japanese culture—in a new light. The sense of dejection that weighed on him could help him let go of his need for recognition and success: *Blessed are those who mourn: the sadness that things don't go as one would like is not the real sadness—and yet the saying "blessed are those who mourn" is true . . . namely, blessed are those for whom things repeatedly go wrong, for then they suffer and are gradually peeled away.*[6]

On the one hand, he considered returning to the Tokyo Settlement to care for the poor and marginalized of Japanese consumer society. On the other hand, he was increasingly drawn to a contemplative life and considered joining a contempla-

---

[3] January 20, 1955.
[4] January 21, 1955.
[5] January 25, 1955.
[6] July 27, 1955.

tive order such as the Carthusians. In this situation, he made the decision to engage more deeply and comprehensively than before in the practice of Zen. The motive was twofold: on the one hand, Zen practice corresponded to his longing for a contemplative life and his desire *to participate in the nature of God—infinite bliss.*[7] On the other hand, from conversations with Zen monks, he had the impression that they were interested in Christianity. Lassalle's friend, the Zen monk Fukuhara Eigan, who was the priest at Kokutaiji, a temple near Hiroshima, had repeatedly said, *Zen no ne ni katoriku no tsukeru, u katoriku no neni Zazen,* that is, combining Catholicism with the roots of Zen and Zen with the roots of Catholicism—of course without grasping *the supernatural in Catholicism,*[8] as Lassalle noted in his diary. Participating in Zen practices and developing a deeper understanding of Zen was also missionary work, Lassalle thought.

His interest in Zen was not based on any kind of exoticism but a result of his personal spiritual path and his work as a Jesuit and missionary in Japan. Although he was irritated by the fact that Zen monks were allowed to marry, the very Zen monks and Zen masters who particularly impressed him—such as Genshu Watanabe, the abbot of Sojiji in Yokohama, and Harada Roshi (1871–1961)–repeatedly regretted this circumstance in conversations with him. Buddhist monks in Japan were allowed to marry since the mid-nineteenth century, an innovation by the Meiji rulers to curb the influence of Buddhist monasteries. Married monks were given a temple as a benefice, and their sons became monks again to inherit the temple from their fathers. For Zen people like Watanabe or Harada, these were signs of decadence in the monastic way of life.

---

[7]April 6, 1955.
[8]April 6, 1955.

For Lassalle, the conclusion was obvious: Zen demonstrated a way of life similar to Christian ascetic practice, a spiritual path similar to mysticism, and made statements about the desired experience of transcendence similar to those of Christian mysticism. This suggested a similar purpose in life. On this premise, he immersed himself deeper and deeper in the practice of Zen for the next thirty years until his death. This repeatedly led him into personal and institutional conflicts, but it did not deter him from his path.

Lassalle contacted the Sojiji in Yokohama and arranged with Genshu Watanabe's assistant to come to the monastery in the summer for a week of Zen practice. And in June, Lassalle attended a sesshin in Obama, a small town on the west coast of Japan, with Harada Sogaku Roshi, one of the great Zen masters of the twentieth century. Harada Roshi had a profound reputation as a critic of the dilution of the monastic tradition that had occurred in the wake of Japan's modernization, and he was also skeptical of the spiritual practice of Soto-shu, to which he belonged.

The crux of his criticism was the question of *kensho* or *satori*. Both literally mean "insight into the nature of the self" and are usually translated as "enlightenment" in Western publications. This must be understood in the context of the Buddhist tradition. *Kensho* is the sudden realization of the Absolute, the momentary cessation of all egoistic and self-referential boundaries—the "death of the small self"—and the experience that everything in the world, including one's own existence, is impermanent, interdependent, and without inherent existence (and therefore "empty"). It is an experience of liberation, as when a heavy burden is lifted from one's shoulders or when all obstacles suddenly disappear. Those who have experienced *kensho* or *satori* have touched the deepest ground of reality and are on their way to overcoming the wheel of rebirth. The archetype of this experience is the "awakening" of the Buddha, who is said to have been liberated and awakened from the cycle of greed, hatred, and delusion.

There are different ways of interpreting this experience in the Buddhist tradition, and different schools of Buddhism use different terms for it. Mahayana Buddhism, for example, uses the term "Buddha nature." In the Zen tradition, it is often said that "all beings have Buddha nature," that is, the Absolute is present in all beings, not just humans. According to the Soto tradition of Zen, Zen practice actualizes Buddha nature, so that the practice itself is already enlightenment. According to the Rinzai tradition, however, practice is necessary to gain sudden insight into Buddha nature, and this insight is then refined through further practice. Harada Roshi belonged to the Soto-shu, but he had also practiced with Rinzai masters and tried to synthesize the two traditions. In particular, he adopted the Rinzai tradition's emphasis on the experience of *kensho* or *satori*, and his uncompromising teaching style and reputation as a strict and demanding Zen master attracted many people, Zen monks from both schools as well as lay people. Harada Roshi was a Japanese of the older generation, both in terms of the rigors of monastic practice and a clear tendency toward nationalism and militarism.[9]

When Hugo Lassalle first came to Hosshinji, Harada Roshi was already in his late eighties and was primarily interested in helping the people who came to him on their path to enlightenment. "Truly enlightened Zen bonzes are not proud; on the contrary, they are very humble and kind people. Anyone who lives in a strict Zen monastery for any length of time will experience this. There is a spirit of goodwill and love there that is hard to find elsewhere. And yet, the Zen masters are terribly strict with their disciples. There are beatings and scoldings without

---

[9] Brian D. Victoria, *Zen at War*, 2nd ed. (Rowman & Littlefield, 2006).

end, so that disciples often lose the courage to approach their master,"[10] wrote Lassalle in his first book, *Zen: Way to Enlightenment*. Although no specific name is mentioned, this was a description of Harada Roshi.

It was in this austere and concentrated atmosphere that Hugo Lassalle began his Zen path with a seven-day sesshin. Sesshin literally means "gathering of the heart-mind." *Morning three o'clock start of the sesshin* with the beating of a drum and the ringing of a clear bell to awaken the participants. Half an hour later, everyone is sitting on their cushions in the zendo. Three strokes of the large bell mark the beginning of the first forty-minute period of zazen. At the end of the sitting period, everyone slides off their seats, bows, and then

Harada Daiun Sogaku Roshi (1871–1961), abbot of Hosshin-ji (Obama, Fukui Prefecture). First Zen master of Fr. Enomiya-Lassalle. He was a Soto monk who trained also with Rinzai masters, combining methods of both Zen schools in his training.

walks several times clockwise around the long and short sides of the room, one after the other, at a slow pace. Then, the next period of zazen begins. During the sesshin, silence prevails, and the sound of bells, drums, and claves marks the entire program. The meals follow a clear ritual, and the food is simple: rice gruel in the morning, rice with vegetables and miso soup

[10] Hugo M. Enomiya-Lassalle, *Zen-Weg zur Erleuchtung* (Herder, 1960), 31.

at noon, and leftovers in the evening. In the morning, there is *samu*, or work time: cleaning the temple, preparing vegetables, gardening—whatever is necessary to maintain the place and the people is done as much as possible by the participants, and this work is part of the Zen practice. Once a day, there is a lecture, *teisho*, and several times a day, there is an opportunity for a ritual conversation with the master, *dokusan*.

Unlike the others who lived in the *zendo*, Hugo Lassalle was given his own room, where he celebrated the Eucharist daily. For the beginners, to which Hugo Lassalle belonged, there was an introduction in the morning and the evening during the first three days, and it was not until the evening of the fourth day that they visited the roshi for the first time. The main purpose of this visit was to clarify the motives for practicing Zen. The classification followed a ladder of motives established by Keizan Jōkin (1268–1325), the fourth patriarch of Soto Zen in Japan. Harada Roshi presented the whole thing as a kind of school system. The first level was Bompu-Zen, or kindergarten Zen, which was practiced to improve concentration and health. Gedo-Zen was "sitting in absorption," as practiced in other religions, such as yoga or Christian contemplation. Gedo-Zen was also used to develop *joriki*, the special abilities that can be developed through intensive practice of mental concentration. Shojo-Zen—equated with the meditation practice of Theravada, the form of Buddhism practiced in Southeast Asia— was the elementary school and served to achieve one's own inner peace. The goal of Daijo-Zen, the high school in Harada Roshi's classification, was "insight into one's innermost nature and the realization of the Great Way in everyday life."[11] The crowning achievement was Saijojo-Zen, which Harada Roshi described as the equivalent of a university: Here one sits, "if

---

[11] Philip Kapleau, ed., *The Three Pillars of Zen. Teaching, Practice and Enlightenment* (Vintage Books, 1989).

practiced correctly, with the firm conviction that zazen is the realization of one's own immaculate True Nature, and at the same time one sits with the firm belief that the day will come when, exclaiming 'Ah, that's it,' one will clearly recognize this True Nature."[12]

In answer to the roshi's question, Lassalle chose "the university," but the roshi questioned the Jesuit priest's sincerity. In response, Lassalle went back to elementary school. All those who had enrolled in the highest level were given the koan "Mu" to practice. *At the last session in the evening, they were instructed to shout from the bottom of their bellies at the sound of the bell and to continue shouting until the bell rang again. They did it like maniacs for about ten minutes. It was deafening. I thought to myself: this method would have been appropriate eight hundred years ago.*[13] The loud shouting of the syllable "Mu"—the Sino-Japanese word for "no" or "nothing"—was one of the special features of Hosshinji and was intended to deepen the practice. Everything about the sesshin environment was designed to bring people to satori. The *jiki-jitsu*, the monk in charge of the zendo, repeatedly shouted and cursed at the meditators during the individual sessions to spur them on to a greater commitment to the practice. The *kyosaku*, the so-called warning stick, a flattened wooden stick used to hit dozing meditators on specific acupressure points in the shoulder or back area, was used like a whip, Lassalle writes, to urge the practitioners to give their utmost. It was not until the seventh day that the room became a little quieter.

What is satori? How does one get it? Who has it? What changes when you have it? These questions began to preoccupy Lassalle. For example, a woman who was also attending her first sesshin came out of the dokusan room crying and

---

12 Kapleau, *The Three Pillars of Zen.*
13 June 1, 1956.

continued to sniffle for a long time in the zazen hall. At the end of the sesshin, Lassalle heard in the roshi's closing remarks that she had attained satori. Then tea and biscuits were served, still in silence, and finally there was a ceremony in front of the *butsudan*, the altar with the Buddha statue in the center of the zendo.

Hugo Lassalle later recalled this first sesshin with Harada Roshi: "My first experience was that my legs hurt terribly. That was my main experience at first."[14] For Lassalle, the parallels between his own ascetic practice and the practice of Zen lay primarily in the struggle against self-cherishing and the realization of selflessness. *It was also emphasized that in daily life, in all situations and work, one must work in the spirit of zazen, that is, always smashing the ego and practicing muga. Even without zazen, one could achieve satori in this way, especially if the work is more physical.*[15] The extent to which the Buddhist view coincided with the Christian view was a question that remained unanswered and would accompany him for the rest of his life, as would the question of what satori is.

The sesshin had been very demanding, but it had strengthened Lassalle's intention to continue on this path and to let Harada Roshi lead the way; maybe it would work, and then a way could be found to have a Catholic sesshin.

As planned, Lassalle attended a four-day sesshin at Sojiji, the large Soto Zen monastery in Yokohama at the end of July. The discipline was much less strict, the silence was not always maintained, and there was an opportunity for an *ofuro*, a hot bath during the breaks. During *dokusan* with Watanabe Genshu, the eighty-eight-year-old abbot and Zen master, *satori* was not mentioned. Watanabe Roshi was a proponent of "gradual culti-

---

[14] Günter Stachel, ed., *Übung der Kontemplation: Christen gehen den Zen-Weg* (Matthias-Grünewald-Verl, 1988), 15.
[15] June 1, 1956.

vation": the original purity of the mind must be cleansed of the "defilements" of the passions, just as a spring has clear water at its source but then becomes increasingly polluted. Harada Roshi, on the other hand, was an advocate of "sudden enlightenment." However, the two agreed on one point: that in both cases, purity of mind must be sought.[16] Gradual cultivation and sudden enlightenment complement each other in practice.

Zen practice helped Lassalle to concentrate more on his daily prayer and contemplation, and above all, zazen enabled him to somehow come to terms with his deep dissatisfaction with his situation: *to endure what could not be changed,* for example, the administrative work as vicar general and parish priest. Zen practice began to accompany his daily life. Along the way, thoughts arose about how Zen and Christian mysticism might fit together. But the crucial question for him was, how does one attain *kensho*? A profound experience of Zen was a prerequisite for holding *a Catholic sesshin* and being accepted by the Zen monks as an equal interlocutor.

In mid-November, Lassalle retired to Sojiji for nine days of solitary retreat under the guidance of Watanabe Genshu. He practiced seven hours a day and soon experienced *makyo,* the characteristic psychophysiological phenomena that indicate that body and mind are gradually beginning to calm down. He entered a profound stillness in which he felt as if he were mesmerized in *emptiness or darkness* and *could not get out.* Again and again, he fell into a state that he described as "*all opposites are resolved,*" as "*absolute stillness.*" At the end of his stay, Lassalle asked the roshi if the states of calm he had experienced were kensho. Watanabe replied in the negative, saying, in accordance with the Soto Zen tradition, that one already has

---

[16] Paul Demiéville, "Mirror of the Mind," in *Sudden and Gradual: Approaches to Enlightenment in Chinese Thought,* ed. Peter N. Gregory (University of Hawaii Press, 1987), 15.

satori, but that one must evolve in it. *The worst thing is to ever stop . . . You have to keep going, 10 years, 20 years, 30 years.*[17] With the experience of absolute stillness, in which disturbances and doubts disappeared, a new dimension had opened up in Lassalle's life. For himself, in his "private language," Lassalle called this experience kensho, although the roshi had neither tested nor confirmed it. The correspondence between the Zen path and his previous path of Christian mysticism began to emerge more and more clearly for him.

"Nothing to hope for, nothing to fear, nothing to rejoice in, nothing to grieve over": these words of the Spanish mystic St. John of the Cross had always been a maxim of his life. During his retreat at Sojiji, he came across a very similar phrase in the Shobogenzo, the famous writing of the great Japanese Zen master Dogen (1200–1250): "Hate nothing, desire nothing, consider nothing in your heart, grieve for nothing," he read in the Shoji section.[18] *It seems to me that everything in my spiritual life is connected to this, even if it will take some time for everything to fit together well,*[19] he noted in his diary.

The effect of *zazen* was soon apparent: despite the external pressures of his work as parish priest and vicar general, Lassalle was able to devote himself more easily and more intensely to daily prayer. It was easier for him to include all his senses and feelings in prayer instead of limiting it to words and thoughts. Lassalle realized that this way of praying was better suited to the Japanese than the usual forms. In addition, this way of praying with all the senses and feelings was well suited to the Ignatian Exercises, where discursive prayer is used to make the life of Jesus present with all senses, thoughts, and feelings, as if one were a contemporary witness of the events.

---

[17] October 20, 1956.
[18] The source in the diaries is "Iwanami tom. 3." For John of the Cross, see "Ascent of Mount Carmel," Book 1.
[19] October 24, 1956.

One of Lassalle's Zen acquaintances from Sojiji, a man named Komoda, gave him an article describing how people are largely determined by the six senses (in Buddhism, thinking is also considered a sense) and by their consciousness, which is bound to the objects of the senses. The "storehouse consciousness" (*alaya vijnana*), which according to Buddhist Yogacara philosophy is the deepest and supraindividual level of consciousness, is active but does not direct action. This is what causes disorder and restlessness in people's lives. Zazen, according to Komoda, calms the senses and consciousness and allows the storehouse consciousness to come into action. Lassalle interpreted the "storehouse consciousness" as *a kind of subconscious* on which the senses of the Zen practitioner should be focused instead of on objects of the external world. Lassalle found that this had significant similarities to the "peeling off" of Christian mysticism, in which the senses are detached from worldly objects, and one arrives at a "night of the senses," as described by St. John of the Cross.

These and other considerations led him to conclude that Zen practice is a "natural means" for preparing the soul for mystical experiences and therefore of great importance, especially for Catholic contemplatives. For the Japanese, it could be a very good way to practice faith, easier to follow than the study of catechism. In addition, the conversations with Watanabe Genshu strengthened Lassalle's conviction that a combination of Zen and Catholicism was a suitable way to stop the decline of traditional values in Japan caused by the emerging industrial and consumer society.

Pedro Arrupe, then provincial of the Japanese Jesuits, gave Lassalle a green light for his plans. In Miyoshi, a place near Hiroshima, Lassalle was able to start a mission project according to his ideas. He also wanted to write a book on Zen and Catholicism in Japanese, and the idea of founding *a Catholic Zen monastery* did not leave him: he considered founding a new order. *If you have a goal, there is also the prospect of realizing it*, he wrote in his diary.[20]

In June 1957, he attended another sesshin at Sojiji, but although he had another experience of deep silence and felt that the roshi confirmed this as enlightenment, an underlying sense of dissatisfaction remained. Two months later, he visited Harada Roshi in Obama to discuss the nature of *kensho* with him again. The roshi—himself a practitioner of the Soto-shu—was very critical: at Sojiji, he said, *kensho* was known only in theory, and at Eiheiji, the main temple of the Soto-shu, even that was unknown.

On October 1, 1957, Lassalle returned to Obama to participate in a sesshin, determined to follow the Zen path under the guidance of Harada Roshi. In the dokusan on the evening of the third day, Harada Roshi gave him the koan Mu as a practice. What is *Mu*? This question should keep the mind focused on "Mu" throughout the practice. The breath should be pressed down hard into the depths of the abdomen, all the way to the absolute (*sunyata*, emptiness). Harada Roshi called this type of breathing, which Lassalle began to practice, *tantei*.

Neither Lassalle nor anyone else attained kensho during this sesshin, but the roshi was very pleased with the intensity and dedication with which Lassalle had practiced.

"A monk asked, 'Does a dog have Buddha nature?', and Joshu replied, 'Mu.'" This koan, in which the great Chinese Ch'an master Chao-chu (Japanese: Joshu) is the main character, presents a paradoxical situation, as all koans do. According to the Mahayana tradition, all living beings have Buddha nature, but Chao-chu (Joshu) answers the monk's question with "Mu," which literally means "has not" or "no." On the level of ordinary, conventional speech, Joshu seems to be saying something that contradicts Buddhist teachings. In the world

---

[20] September 27, 1957.

of koans, however, there is no "yes/no" duality, nor are there definitive meanings as in conventional language.

Most koans are anecdotes from the "Golden age of Zen"[21] about encounters between master and disciple, master and master, or even disciple and disciple. In these encounters, "it" occurs between the two interlocutors—the "absolute," "emptiness" (*sunyata*), "Buddha nature." A twentieth-century Zen master clarifies this in his commentary on Joshu's anecdote as follows: "As a true, capable master, Joshu replied 'Mu!' without the slightest hesitation. He threw himself—the whole universe—before the questioner as 'Mu'. There is no Joshu, no world, only 'Mu' . . . It has nothing to do with the dualistic interpretation of yes and no, being and non-being. It is truth itself, the absolute itself"[22]—not captured in conceptual form, but present in the here and now.

In order for a contemporary Zen student to grasp this truth, however, he or she, like all Zen students before, must first forget the conventional ways of knowing. Hugo Lassalle was no different from many other Zen students in this respect: he spent a long time trying to make sense of the koan using images and metaphors. Harada Roshi did not accept these answers in *dokusan* and instructed Lassalle to continue concentrating on Mu with every breath. In *teisho*, his daily Dharma talk, Roshi said that *satori* was the "great emptiness." He did not approve of the experiences Lassalle reported from his week of practice at Sojiji. So, what was *satori* or *kensho*? Lassalle tried his best to find out by talking to people who had more experience with Zen. One of them was Philip Kapleau, an American journalist who had covered the Nuremberg trials of Nazi war criminals and later the war crimes trials in Japan. His experience of war and war crimes

---

[21] John C. H. Wu, *The Golden Age of Zen: Zen Masters of the T'ang Dynasty* (1967).

[22] Shibayama Zenkei, *Zu den Quellen des Zen* (Heyne Verlag,1986), 24.

had led him to doubt the Western humanistic tradition.

Kapleau met D. T. Suzuki (1870–1966), who introduced him to Zen Buddhism, in 1947. He returned to Japan to practice Zen, hoping to find a solution to his problems. Lassalle had met him at Hosshinji at a time when Harada Roshi had just recognized the young American's kensho. Lassalle tried to elicit a description of this experience from Kapleau, but in vain. The difference between the neo-scholastic training that had shaped Lassalle and the worldview of the young American who had just immersed himself in Buddhism was too great. Kapleau said that what Harada recognized as kensho was only the beginning of a long journey. Lassalle's questions about *whether this kensho was the true nature of being* remained unanswered.[23]

Lassalle's friend Komoda, on the other hand, held the classical Soto view of kensho: *Everyone has muishikishin* [nonmind]*, but they don't know it. Through zazen, they come to know that they have it.*[24] Sometime later, Lassalle heard from Ban Tetsugen Roshi, one of Harada Roshi's Dharma successors, that Komoda himself probably did not have *kensho*. During his next *sesshin* at Hosshinji in early June 1958, Lassalle made a new attempt: he asked the roshi whether *kensho* was a kind of psychological ecstasy. In Catholic mystical discourse of the time, this was a term occasionally used to describe mystical experiences. Harada Roshi did not understand what Lassalle was talking about and explained to him what "nothing" was, using words from the Buddhist tradition—which Lassalle again did not understand. Finally, the roshi explained that Buddha or God is located below the navel and is awakened by *tantei*, the intense Zen breath, and demonstrated how to breathe.

---

[23] April 4, 1958.
[24] April 12, 1958.

The questions about *kensho* were not only for Lassalle's own personal orientation. As planned, Lassalle had begun to write a book entitled *Zen: Way to Enlightenment*, which described Lassalle's experiences and suggested that Christians could follow the Zen path as a way to a "natural experience of God." Provincial Pedro Arrupe gave permission for the book to be printed in June 1958, and it was published by Herder Publishing House in Vienna in the fall of 1960 with ecclesiastical permission and a foreword by Cardinal Franz König.

In the fall of 1958, Lassalle prepared a position paper on the practice of Zen for internal discussion within the order, "Declaration on the Postulate on Za-Zen." The method of practice, that is, physical posture and concentration on the breath, "is universal in nature and not bound to any religious creed"[25] and can therefore be separated from Buddhism. It was conducive to the life of prayer and particularly suited to the Japanese. Equanimity and self-control, values highly prized in Japanese culture, were "ultimately derived from this method," and in this respect of "natural virtues" the Japanese were far superior to the Europeans—including the Jesuit Fathers. "They must first be on a par with

Fr. Enomiya-Lassalle in the 1950s.

---

[25] Arch. Prov. VII/4 1958. The following quotes are also taken from this source.

the pagans in natural virtue before they can explain the super-natural [Christianity] to them," Lassalle wrote in the paper.

The result of the internal consultation was very critical, but not fundamentally negative. Zazen should be practiced only as an aid to prayer and self-control, but satori should not be pursued. Lassalle should continue his work in Hiroshima but not go to Tokyo. *They did not want the matter to become too prominent.*[26] Only existing Jesuit facilities were to be used. However, Pedro Arrupe, the provincial, told Lassalle that it would be a good idea to acquire a house for Zen. Lassalle wrote in his diary: *"If God wills it, I will find my way."*[27] So he began to look for a suitable building site for a Catholic Zen retreat house. The fact that the Zen masters he knew attached varying degrees of importance to *the experience* of *kensho* encouraged him not to wait for formal recognition of a *kensho* experience. He wanted to present Zen practice as a way to inner peace and deeper prayer for Christians. And for himself, the practice of "sitting in absorption" revealed more of the deeper dimensions of the Christian tradition. During his annual retreat, his meditation on Jesus's suffering and death for the love of humanity moved him more deeply than ever before. *I'd have to do everything in—I say "in," not just "out of"—love [. . .], in this love that Zen seems to make possible.*[28]

With the support of Provincial Pedro Arrupe, Lassalle was able to realize many of his plans.

In March 1958, he held his first retreat at the Jesuit retreat house in Nagatsuka, near Hiroshima, combining Zen practice with Christian discursive prayer. As is customary in discursive prayer, before each session he outlined "points"—aspects of the Gospel and Christian tradition on which to focus during

---

[26] November 26, 1958.
[27] November 26, 1958.
[28] January 29, 1958.

zazen. It was a demanding twenty-four hours, during which the thirty-eight participants practiced sitting in silence for fifteen sessions of forty minutes each.

He himself kept return-ing to Obama to partici-pate in the sesshin, usually on his BMW motorcycle. Photographs from this period show an elegant and seemingly auda-cious, tall, slender man in a leather jacket stand-ing next to his vehicle. During these sesshins at Hosshinji, he became friends with Harada Tan-gen (1924–2018), previ-ously a monk and later a roshi at Bukkokuji, a small temple very close to Hosshinji. When Lassalle

Pedro Arrupe, Provincial of the Jesuits in Japan, later Superior General of the Society of Jesus.

practiced zazen in the garden at night after the official practice session, Harada Tangen would sit next to him. Lassalle visited him during his few days of vacation, and Harada Tangen in turn came to Hiroshima for Christmas.

Harada Roshi, now eighty-seven years old, was ready to retire. During the last sesshin in November 1960, which Lassalle attended, he once again encouraged Lassalle to devote himself fully to solving the koan Mu. *If you achieve kensho, it could be of great significance for Japan,*[29] he said. But Lassalle did not solve the koan during this sesshin either.

---

[29] November 11, 1959.

Shortly thereafter, Lassalle bought a piece of land in Kabe, near Hiroshima, to build a Catholic Zen center. The book *Zen—Way to Enlightenment* was published in early 1960, received positive reviews on Vatican Radio, and aroused great interest in Europe. On New Year's Eve 1960, Lassalle summed up his year with great optimism: "*Forward!*" he wrote in his diary. "*In any case, I must look back on this year with gratitude, despite all its mistakes and failures. [. . . Deo Gratias!*"[30]

A few days later, shortly after the New Year, Provincial Arrupe informed Lassalle of a letter from Rome signed by Father Janssens, the superior general of the Jesuits. The "Zen method" was not to be taught to Jesuits or laymen, and the book *Zen—Way to Enlightenment* was not to be published (although it had already been printed and sold well). Lassalle himself, however, was allowed to continue practicing Zen and to develop a method *adapted to the Japanese way of discursive prayer.*[31] At first thoughts raced through Lassalle's head. Should he give up everything related to Zen out of loyalty to the order? The annual retreat at the end of January offered a good opportunity to collect his thoughts. The Zen path is a path of self-realization, and this is in accordance with the teachings of the Church Fathers and the Christian mystics of the Middle Ages. *For God is in the soul of the righteous. So if we go deep within ourselves, we must find Him within ourselves.* To do this, we must abandon *all sensual perceptions and philosophical conclusions*[32] and become still within ourselves. *The physical posture of zazen predisposes people on a physiological level to become still, which is a prerequisite for self-realization and the realization of God. It is really just a matter of physiology. Everything else should remain Christian for us. Of course, this*

---

[30] December 31, 1960.
[31] January 11, 1961.
[32] January 20, 1961.

may be difficult to understand for those who have not experienced it.[33] The goal of Zen, according to Harada Roshi, is *satori*, the experience of the absolute. Lassalle concluded that the goal of *zazen* for Christians is the experience of God.

Pedro Arrupe, the provincial, agreed with these thoughts. He thought that Lassalle should build the planned meditation house in order to practice Zen to the extent permitted by Rome. The house in Kabe was finally inaugurated on December 17, 1961, and Lassalle's old friend, the Zen priest Fukuhara Eigan from Hiroshima, gave it the name *Shinmeikutsu*, "Cave of Divine Darkness." The new bishop of Hiroshima, Noguchi, also supported Lassalle's Zen work. And Father Bruno Bitter, his old friend from his student days, advised him to follow his conscience, which meant to keep going. Nevertheless, Lassalle found himself in inner crises again and again because of the Roman prohibition. He saw the spread of Zen as his mission, and the thought that his life was coming to an end—he was sixty-two at the time—drove him forward. On the other hand, he also saw his difficulties as an opportunity for spiritual growth: *God wants to humble my pride, and he uses my superiors to do it,* [34] he reflected self-critically.

An explanatory letter arrived from Rome from the vicar general of the order, who knew and respected Father Lassalle personally. The accusations of the censors—two in Japan and two in Rome—were so severe that he "could not understand why the book was allowed to be printed." Vicar General Swain promised to resolve the matter quickly within the order. "I do not see any other way to proceed in a matter which may otherwise be taken out of our hands and judged by the Holy Office [now the Congregation for the Doctrine of the Faith],"[35] he wrote.

---

[33] January 26, 1961.
[34] January 23, 1961.
[35] Dated Rome, April 30, 1961, unpublished.

All this happened in the run-up to the Second Vatican Council. Lassalle was to accompany the bishop of Hiroshima there and use the opportunity to try to clarify the Zen question in Rome, said Pedro Arrupe. And Lassalle immediately made further plans: a trip to Mount Athos, and then to India, Burma, and Thailand to study the relationship between Christian and Asian mysticism on the spot. On June 17, 1960, Lassalle left Tokyo for Europe.

6

What Is Enlightenment?

❧

In Rome, Hugo Lassalle first sought out Jesuits he knew from earlier days, who were now participating in the Council as cardinals, to discuss the censored book with them. Cardinal Joseph Frings (1887–1987) of Cologne—whom Lassalle had met in 1957 during a visit to Japan with Soto Zen Master Watanabe Genshu at Sojiji—remained skeptical. Even the talks in Rome with Cardinal Augustin Bea (1881–1968)—whom he knew from his studies in Valkenburg—and with Cardinal Paolo Marella (1895–1984), who had lived in Japan for many years and supported Lassalle's missionary ideas, were of no avail. Only a conversation with the Jesuit Superior General Father Janssens (1889–1964), brought Lassalle a step further.

Janssens saw the question very pragmatically: the adaptation of Catholic Christianity to non-European structures remained a task, and whoever began it would *always* encounter *difficulties*.[1] Although the censors' verdict was binding on him, a new edition of the book in a revised form was conceivable. Lassalle should be given access to the censors' judgments, which, by

---

[1] July 1, 1962.

85

the way, should have happened long ago. Nothing more could be done at that time.

In August, everything in Rome came to a standstill because of the summer vacation. Lassalle traveled to Mount Athos in Greece, the center of Eastern Church mysticism with a tradition dating back to early Christianity. In Istanbul, he obtained a five-day visa for Mount Athos from the Orthodox Patriarch. The day after his arrival, the foundation of the monastery was celebrated at the Lavran Monastery, and Lassalle was fascinated by the liturgy, with the monks' choirs rising and falling in waves, the many candles, and the incense. "The whole celebration trembled with holy joy, which burst into such exuberant rejoicing during the singing of the Hosanna that it was as if the heavenly Jerusalem were really descending to earth at that moment."[2] He was also impressed by the fact that there were no class distinctions during the liturgy and afterward at the agape, the communal meal after the service, and that beggars, monks, and lay people sat side by side. The spirituality of the Eastern Church, he noted, anticipates in the liturgy the coming kingdom of God, in which there are no longer any differences or oppositions between people; it is "at the same time an indication that it is not law but love that should regulate life."[3] However, he found no information about the mystical experience of the "Tabor light" reported by Eastern Church spirituality. For the monks in the monasteries knew little of their mystical tradition. Only a few monks who lived outside the monasteries in hermitages were able to give Lassalle information about the practice of the Jesus Prayer. However, no one knew anything about the "Tabor light," the experience of enlightenment; the few hermits who had actually experienced it would avoid the

---

[2] Hugo M. Enomiya-Lassalle, *Zen-Buddhismus,* 3rd ed. (Bachem, 1974), 360.

[3] Enomiya-Lassalle, *Zen-Buddhismus,* 360

monasteries, it was said. It was only later, while reading the *Philokalia*, a collection of texts by the Fathers of the Eastern Church, that Lassalle discovered parallels between the Jesus Prayer and the practice of Zen.

By the early 1960s, most European colonies in Asia and Africa had gained political independence and were members of the UN. The emerging "global community of states" and the impending economic and cultural conflicts were the topics of the Salzburg University Weeks, a renowned yearly summer school, in 1962. Lassalle was asked to speak on "The Mystical Solidarity of the West with the Religions of Greater Asia." There were many people in the audience who had been practicing yoga or similar disciplines for a long time, and after the lecture there was a lively discussion; *the difficulties the censors had with my book were not mentioned,*[4] Lassalle noted in his diary.

During the Salzburg University Weeks, he met, among others, the Benedictine monk Cyrill von Korvin-Krasinksy, who gave a lecture on "The Entitlement of Poor Peoples to the Abundance of Rich Peoples." He was a well-traveled and experienced man who had just written a book on Tibetan medicine. He and Lassalle became good friends.

Lassalle used the time until the beginning of the first session of the Vatican Council in early October 1962 to travel for various purposes. Sometimes, this involved the finances of the diocese of Hiroshima, at other times, he visited his mother and sisters in Hildesheim, but above all, he sought out men who were concerned with questions similar to his own, such as the Jesuit theologian and later cardinal Jean Danielou (1905–1974) in Paris, who argued that there were connections between the Prayer of the Heart of the Eastern Church and Buddhist meditation practices. The Indologist and philosopher

---

[4]August 11, 1962.

Olivier Lacombe (1904–2001) confirmed Lassalle's view that there is a "natural mysticism," that is, mystical experiences that anyone can have, regardless of religious affiliation. For Lassalle, this was a major step beyond the prevailing view in Catholic circles of the time, which held that mystical experiences were either "supernatural," that is, somehow fitting into the Christian framework of "supernatural revelation," or false and, therefore, evil. By chance, he also met the Buddhist monk Walpola Rahula (1907–1997) from Sri Lanka in Paris, who explained to him that the miracles of Jesus were not supernatural at all, because Christ had been a yogi and therefore naturally capable of performing miracles.

The Spanish Jesuit and writer Carlos M. Staehlin in Madrid, on the other hand, argued that the opposition between "natural" and "supernatural" didn't make sense. Either one has experienced ultimate reality or one has not, said the Jesuit, who himself had practiced yoga for a long time. The renowned Oxford religious scholar R. C. Zaehner (1913–1974), on the other hand, believed that one should speak of "nature mysticism" rather than "natural mysticism." After a very cordial conversation with Zaehner, Lassalle left Oxford at three in the morning to return to London to catch an early flight to Cologne. His destination was the Carthusian monastery in Cologne, for one of his ideas was to return to Japan as a Carthusian monk in order to resolve his problems with Rome and the Jesuit order. This idea preoccupied him again and again, and whenever he came near a Carthusian monastery on his many travels—in Grenoble, for example—he spent a few days in the concentrated silence of these monasteries, which appealed to him very much.

He arrived in Rome just in time to attend the solemn opening of the Vatican Council on October 11. The first session of the Council ended on December 8, 1962, and showed that "traditionalists" and "progressives" could not agree on issues such as liturgy and the Bible as a text of revelation. On the basis of their pastoral experience, the representatives of non-European countries, in particular, argued strongly for an *aggiornamento*, an adaptation of the Catholic tradition to the changed situation of the world. The very fact that the Council had been convened and that bishops from all continents were participating at this time showed how much the Catholic Church had changed since the end of the nineteenth century.

In Madrid that summer, Pedro Arrupe had told Lassalle that no one in Rome was in a position to judge the issues surrounding Zen. Arrupe believed that the book would probably not be approved, but that Lassalle could apply the Zen method to Japanese Buddhists under the supervision of theologians in Tokyo who would evaluate his work. After Lassalle finally received the written judgments on his book, he was advised to consult the theologian Johannes Lotz (1903–1992), a Jesuit and German himself. Lotz was a leading expert on Scholasticism, but he was also interested in meditation and knew Karlfried Graf Dürckheim's books on Zen. Lotz saw no problem with the whole "Zen question"; on the contrary, he saw parallels between the theology of Thomas Aquinas and what he had read in Dürckheim. In his opinion, Lassalle had gotten into trouble with his book because he had not explained clearly enough the differences between Buddhists and Christians in their interpretation of the experience of meditation.

In addition to all these activities related to Zen, Lassalle's main task in Europe was to take care of Bishop Noguchi (1909–1997). Over Christmas, Lassalle accompanied Bishop Noguchi to Berlin. As Japanese citizens, the two were able to travel to the eastern part of the city, which was under Soviet control; the wall separating the eastern part had been built only a year ago in August 1961. On their way back, they saw three men on the East German side of the wall waving to their wives in the West. Lassalle learned that *one of these couples was celebrating their silver wedding anniversary that day.*[5]

---

[5] December 26, 1962.

On the last day of his stay in Berlin, a woman named Gerta Ital (1904–1988) called to say she wanted to visit him. She told him that she had devoured Lassalle's book on Zen but then heard from her bookseller that the priest had fallen victim to the atomic bomb. She had read in the newspaper about the visit of the two Japanese in Berlin and thought that Father Enomiya might be a relative of the deceased. So, she called and made an appointment. The priest, Gerta Ital later recalled, was "a tall, slender, almost athletic figure . . . his age was indefinable. For this priest, whose blond head bore a striking resemblance to the stern, handsome face of the famous royal horseman in Bamberg Cathedral, also possessed the same timelessness in his expression and, later in conversation, sometimes the same distant gaze." She asked if the priest might be related to the deceased. "A surprised, searching look rested on me for a long time, but then the priest said seriously, 'Yes.' 'And you knew him?' Again I received a serious 'yes' in reply." She said she had hoped to find in this priest a "kind advisor" for her Zen path. The news of his death hit her hard. "There was a long pause while I held Father's deep gaze. Then he said: 'I am Enomiya-Lassalle.'"

Lassalle encouraged Gerta Ital to go to Japan. "Go with God. You will reach your goal," he told her as she left.[6] She later received permission to teach Zen and wrote several books about her experiences in Japan.

In early January 1963, Lassalle traveled to the Black Forest to visit Karlfried Graf Dürckheim (1896–1988). Dürckheim had founded a center for "initiatory therapy" in Rütte in 1951, integrating Zen practice with "bodywork" in a therapeutic method designed to heal emotional wounds and open the way to spiritual experience.

---

[6] Gerta Ital, *Der Meister, die Mönche und ich*, 4th ed. (Sierra Taschenbuch,1966), 35–37.

Fr. Enomiya-Lassalle with Karlfried Graf Dürckheim-Montmartin. In 1952 Dürckheim had founded Initiatic Therapy, the first transpersonal therapy. He also introduced Zen practice in this context. (Photo most likely from the 1970s.)

Lassalle had made an appointment, and the secretary told Dürckheim that a certain Mr. Enomiya wanted to talk to him about Zen. Years later, Dürckheim reported, "I was told that the tall, slender man was dressed very simply, like a wanderer . . . He was extremely modest and knew the art of listening. Surprisingly, he knew a lot about Zen. I advised him to go to Japan to deepen his knowledge and learn the language so that he could absorb the spirit of Zen from within. This Mr. Enomiya replied, 'I have lived in Japan for thirty years, and I speak Japanese fluently.' Then I said to him, 'Then you must definitely go and see the famous Father Lassalle; this man is very skilled in Zen and also has a great knowledge of the Japanese mentality.' There was a pause. Then this Mr. Enomiya said, 'I am Father Lassalle.'"[7] The modesty with which Hugo Lassalle presented

---

[7] Gerhard Wehr, *Karlfried Graf Dürckheim: Ein Leben im Zeichen der Wandlung* (Kösel, 1988), 217.

himself astonished Count Dürckheim for years to come.

Before his final departure from Rome, Lassalle had another conversation with the superior general about the use of Zen practice as a method for himself and for *mature priests*, in which the latter clearly told him that *he did not want to stop the matter*. In the seventeenth century the Jesuits had been forbidden by the Vatican to integrate Chinese expressions and traditions into their missionary efforts. This rite controversy over the adaption of Christianity to Chinese culture had done enough damage, said Father Janssens.[8] So Lassalle set out in good spirits on his journey, which took him to Israel in mid-January, initially for five days, following in the footsteps of Jesus. But the real destination of the trip was India and Thailand, where he hoped to learn more about yoga, Buddhist spirituality, and its possible connection to Christianity.

In India, Lassalle was irritated by the unfamiliar density and proximity of contrasts. India was an Asian country, but very different from Japan—on the one hand, there was the obvious poverty, on the other, the religious devotion and fervor of the Hindus.

Lassalle visited the historical sites of Buddhism in Sarnath and Bodh Gaya; he traveled to Benares, the spiritual heart of India, and to Calcutta (today Kolkata), to Mother Teresa. Above all, he sought Indian spirituality. This led him first to the Lonavla Yoga College and the Santa Cruz Yoga Institute in Bombay. At both places, attempts were made to study the physiological effects of yoga. Lassalle found this interesting but not really satisfying. A visit to Dr. Vinod, an old guru who taught Shabda Yoga, gave him more insight. The white-bearded old man said that every person has his own special note that he must find in order to attain enlightenment. Then he said that Lassalle's last birth had been in India and that he

---

[8] January 14, 1963.

had died at the age of twenty-seven from overexertion during spiritual practices. In this life, his visitor had been on a spiritual path since the age of nineteen, the old man said. *When he heard that I was Catholic, he said that I had become one with Christ (or something like that) and that Christ now had to be universalized in me.*[9]

Lassalle first heard from the Jesuits in Bombay, where he was staying, about attempts to unite Indian and Christian spirituality in India beginning in the late 1940s. In southern India, in Tamil Nadu, the Benedictine Henri Le Saux—his Indian name was Abhishik-tananda—had founded the Shantivanam Ash-ram in 1950, and in Kerala another Bene-dictine, Jules Mon-chanin, had founded

Henri Le Saux (Swami Abhishiktananda).

the Kurisumala Ashram, which, after his death, was taken over by a young English Benedictine, Bede Griffiths, who, like Hugo Lassalle himself, is one of the great figures of Christian dialogue with the traditions of Asia.

Bede Griffiths, who in 1968 became head of Shantivanam, encouraged Lassalle in his conviction that in order to engage in dialogue with Hindus or Buddhists, it was necessary to have the same experience as they did: *the experience of the infinite,*

---

[9] January 25, 1963.

which is open to God—satori, as Lassalle himself translated it.[10] In Delhi, he then met the Swiss diplomat and religious scholar Jacques-Albert Cuttat (1909–1989) at the Swiss embassy. Cuttat was very skeptical about a dialog of experience. Enlightenment was not a natural process, he said, and as a Christian one would encounter great emotional difficulties as a result. As a cautionary example, he cited the example of the Benedictine Henri Le Saux (Abhishiktananda), one of the great pioneers of dialogue with the religions of Asia.

The stay in India did not satisfy Lassalle's interest very much. A brief stay in Rangoon (today Yangon), the capital of Burma (today Myanmar), brought him further. He visited the centers of the two important meditation teachers of Theravada Buddhism, U Ba Khin and Mahasi Sayadaw. And in Bangkok, the capital of Thailand, he also spoke with various meditation teachers. The difference between the Zen method and the Theravada practice became clear to him. In Theravada practice, feelings or physical sensations are made the object of meditation, whereas in Zen this is not the case as there is no object. However, the same thing happens in both paths of practice, namely, that the mind and desires gradually come to rest—and in this respect, these paths correspond to Christian mysticism.[11] If one disregarded the specific religious content and considered the different methods phenomenologically, there seemed to be a common spiritual basis for all these paths, Lassalle noted.

This, however, was not the opinion of the Jesuit fathers in Tokyo, who had to pass judgment on Lassalle's Zen project. In mid-May, Lassalle received from this committee a set of "standards" ("normae") for the practice of Zen, which prohibited everything that the Jesuit general, Father Janssens, had

---

[10] January 30, 1963.
[11] *Cf.* Enomiya-Lassalle, *Zen-Buddhismus*, 126ff.

promised to agree to in a conversation. According to these standards, Hugo Lassalle and other Jesuit priests were only allowed to practice Zen under the supervision of their superior, who, of course, knew nothing about Zen. If lay people wanted to receive an introduction to Zen from Lassalle, they needed permission from the local bishop. Among his fellow brothers, he found some who understood his desperate situation, but none of them could understand that Zen practice had become part of Lassalle's spiritual life. And even respected experts on Buddhism, such as Father Heinrich Dumoulin, were far from understanding Lassalle's insight into *the necessity of integrating the religious tradition* [of Zen]*, insofar as it contains positive values.*[12] *So all I can say is that I will proceed as Father General wishes (according to my conscience) and concern myself as little as possible with the normae, insofar as they restrict the matter more than the General intended.*[13]

The difficulty lay in the fact that Lassalle had not only learned the Japanese language and culture but that through his practice of Zen, he had entered into the heart[14] of this foreign culture and tradition, not as an observer but as a participant. Nevertheless, he did not want to renounce or deny his origins and identity as a Christian and Jesuit. The difficulties that arose were mainly related to the fact that he had to rearticulate his sense of self in such a way that he could live in both traditions. This was an extremely difficult task and, at the same time, an undertaking that unsettled many of his religious brothers because it could challenge their own sense of self. However, people who were more distant from the church found Lassalle's path and his search for a deeper spirituality very inspiring. The example of the Jesuit and scientist Teilhard de Chardin encouraged

---

[12] November 15, 1963.
[13] May 12, 1963.
[14] Letter June 16, 1961 (unpublished).

Lassalle to proceed further. Teilhard had advocated a connection between Darwin's theory of evolution and the basic ideas of Christian theology; he, too, had been silenced by the church, but he had not been deterred from his path while remaining anchored in the church.

The book *Zen—Way to Enlightenment* had meanwhile been reviewed by the Roman censors, who remained anonymous, for necessary changes in the text. They stated that Zen was acceptable to Christians as a "physical-psychological method," that is, "stripped of its Buddhist content." The method, they continued, was "neither prayer nor anything spiritual" and therefore could never be a substitute for Christian meditation, "which must always somehow enter into dialogue with God." It served "the skilful exploitation of natural forces," but, according to the correction to Lassalle's text, it lacked both "the imitation of Christ as the way and immediate goal, which goes beyond natural virtue, and the deliberate orientation toward the love of God as the ultimate goal." With these and a number of other changes, the book could be republished in German. Of course, the readers of the book had very different interests from the theologians. In one case, for example, a man asked for advice because he could not sit without pain. Lassalle was able to offer a solution: "Recently, some Zen masters have tried to make a specially designed chair that places the body in a position similar to that of the *hanka* [heel seat]," he wrote, and procured the man with a meditation stool via Yasutani Roshi.[15] This was probably the first example of this piece of meditation furniture, which is now widely used throughout the Christian world.

At the end of July 1964, the first sesshin was held in the newly built Zen retreat house in Kabe-Shinmeikutsu. The participants, eleven Japanese Christians who had known Lassalle

---

[15] June 7, 1963.

for a long time, subsequently founded a *Sanzenkai*, an association of Zen practitioners, which existed until the house in Kabe had to be sold to an electricity company in the 1970s.

Aerial view of Shinmeikutsu, Fr. Enomiya-Lassalle's Zen Retreat House in the Akigawa valley near Tokyo.

Through all these years, Hugo Lassalle attended sesshins at Hosshinji every few months in search of the answer to the *muji*, the koan Mu. Sessui Roshi, Harada Roshi's successor, repeatedly encouraged him to persevere. *In everyday life, everything is muji. The self, everything you hear and see. One should have this belief, therefore everything one does is only for the moment.*[16]

However, Lassalle could not reconcile this view with the theological framework he had acquired through his upbringing and education, which was strongly influenced by rational concepts and arguments. On the other hand, this rational approach

---

[16] July 5, 1963.

to the world was becoming increasingly alien to him. *In any case, logical reasoning has long since ceased to work for me. Perhaps one could say that I need to enter a new mode of consciousness.*[17] This was compounded by a clear awareness of his own imperfections. It was a passage through purgatory, a journey through the labyrinth in which the center seems close for a moment but then disappears again into the distance. Until the beginning of the modern age, the image of the labyrinth was used for meditation in church rooms, as an image of man's path to God. Hugo Lassalle sometimes felt that he was walking through such a labyrinth on his way to the center: *I have to go to nothingness.*[18]

But it was impossible to foresee how long the journey would take; *once you have taken the leap, you cannot stop halfway.*[19] And once you have traveled a certain distance, there is no turning back—you will never forget the experiences you have made along the way, you are no longer the same person. Lassalle often mentioned this in his lectures during his sesshins in Europe.

Harada Roshi had passed away in November 1961, and Hugo Lassalle began to look for a new Zen teacher. A friend advised him to attend a sesshin with Yasutani Roshi, one of Harada Roshi's Dharma heirs. Harada Roshi's Zen had had a very militant tone, but Lassalle found the sesshin with Yasutani Roshi (1885–1973) to be *worse than anything* he had ever experienced at Hosshinji. Every day, the blows with the kyosaku became more violent, the shouts of encouragement from the monks in charge and the "Mu" of the practitioners became louder. *But in the end, no one achieved kensho.*[20] Two months

---

[17] September 4, 1963.
[18] August 21, 1963.
[19] June 15, 1964.
[20] August 29, 1964.

later, Lassalle attended a sesshin at a Zen nunnery. Here, the practice involved less physical effort and more application of the heart, and the Nagasawa Roshi said that the traditional Mahayana Buddhist vow to save all sentient beings, recited several times a day in every Zen temple, was essential if kensho was to be of any use. She dismissed Lassalle's questions in *dokusan* and told him to always have a *kokoro ni asobi koto*, "a playful heart." The *sesshin* benefited Lassalle, but he had reservations about attending more often, since it was a nunnery, *even though it was a harmless thing and many men attended.*[21]

With each step toward the center of the labyrinth, Lassalle was presented with new experiences. During the October sesshin with Sessui Roshi in Obama, he was overcome with deep joy on the last night—but the expected breakthrough remained out of reach. The Rohatsu sesshin in December was bitterly cold, the paper windows provided no insulation, and Lassalle shivered. The roshi sent him into town to buy warm clothes and had warm drinks brought to his room. But again, the question of "Mu" remained unsolved. After this sesshin, Lassalle decided to give up his intense focus on satori. At the same time, however, it became increasingly clear to him that *Zen is life.*[22]

For the now sixty-six-year-old, the quest for enlightenment also had a very existential aspect. He had long been preoccupied with the question of what happens after death. Even if no human being could give a definitive answer, since God's perfection transcends all human conceptualization, it must be possible to live here and now from this other, perfected reality. Lassalle realized that Zen and Christian mysticism agreed on this point. The fear of death became for him an indication *that he should live in the ground,*[23] in the nonplace, where there

---

[21] December 30, 1964.
[22] December 30, 1964.
[23] April 24, 1965.

is no difference between life and death. His longing for a life grounded in zazen, in the "center," thus became even more urgent.

In order to rethink the relationship between Zen and Christian mysticism, also on the basis of his experiences on Mount Athos, in India, Burma, and Thailand, he worked for a long time on a new book, which was then published under the title *Zen Buddhism*. It contained not only a detailed description of Zen practice, but, above all, showed where connections could be found in the Christian tradition for an interpretation of Zen practice. Lassalle found fundamental parallels in early Christianity and in mystics such as Meister Eckhart, Bonaventure, Teresa of Ávila, and John of the Cross, as well as in the Jesus Prayer of the Eastern Church.

He believed that a new order should be founded for the practice of Zen by Christians, an order that would be *entirely Japanese* in its way of life and open to men and women, married and unmarried. The ideal of the order should be the pursuit of Christian perfection, and it should be open only to people who truly want to follow the Zen path. Lassalle did not believe that communal living was necessary, but he did believe that members of the order should follow the path of poverty in their daily lives. Lassalle found an example of this way of life in the Dominican priest Shigeto Oshida (1922–2003), who had left the comfortable life of the convent to live in the mountains near Matsumoto. The hut in which he lived was made of discarded materials, and his food came from donations from the inhabitants of the surrounding villages; later, he also had a small rice field that had been lent to him. Poverty and quiet contemplation characterized the life of the small community in Takamori, and even outsiders of Japanese society could find a place here.

Fr. Enimoya Lassalle in his first Zen retreat house in Kabe near Hiroshima, with Japanese Christians, around 1965.

However, the prospects of implementing the plans for a Zen order were slim. Lassalle did receive support from outside sources, such as Cardinal Marella, who visited Hiroshima during a stay in Japan, and the Spanish–Indian religious philosopher and theologian Raimon Panikkar (1918–2010), who visited him during this period. Encouraged by his friend Fukuhara Eigan, the monk at Kokutaiji, Lassalle decided to found a community near Tokyo where Zen and Christianity could be integrated. However, Lassalle received no support for such plans from his Japanese superiors. The young clergy were still trained in traditional Western spirituality, and they were forbidden "to sit zazen-style" while reading the Scriptures. To Lassalle, this seemed to contradict the intentions of the Second Vatican Council: *The Council surely wants seminarians and members of religious orders to be introduced to the traditions of their cultural and religious world from the very first day, and not after they have absorbed the entire Western way of life.*[24]

---

[24] April 17, 1965.

Lassalle wrote to Pedro Arrupe in Rome, who had been elected superior general of the Jesuits in 1965, asking for support in integrating Zen into Christianity. Arrupe gave instructions to revise the "standards/normae." But then Lassalle happened to hear from a fellow Jesuit that the influential Jesuit fathers in the Japanese province were opposed to his Zen plans and that the decision on his case was being postponed again and again. The situation seemed hopeless.

On the one hand, Lassalle felt that it was his life's work to promote the integration of Zen. On the other hand, there were all the obstacles resulting from the situation within the order. The only way out of this situation seemed to Lassalle to be exclaustration, the release from membership in the order's community. In mid-March 1966, he retired to his annual retreat to reflect on the situation. During this time, he suddenly began to use the Latin alphabet in his diary. Until then, he had written in the old Sütterlin script. This clearly shows the depth of the crisis in which the now sixty-eight-year-old found himself, as a new beginning loomed.

Since the circumstances did not change fundamentally, he decided to apply for exclaustration so that he could do something about Zen. *And I believe that the urge comes from God. The inner conflict is sometimes unbearable.* Asking for exclaustration was not an easy decision. *Because leaving the order is the greatest sacrifice of my life,*[25] he wrote in his diary on Holy Saturday, 1966. On Easter Sunday, he wrote to Pedro Arrupe, asking for an "exclaustratio ad tempus" for two or three years. "But I want to make it very clear that at the hour of my death, which is surely not far off, I do not want to have to reproach myself for having refrained from doing what I believed to be

---

[25] April 9, 1966.

God's will for fear of sacrifice in an important matter,"[26] he wrote in the letter.

Arrupe's answer cleared the path for Lassalle: "Your plan for a house in Tokyo is interesting. But it seems best to me that you first discuss it with Father Provincial. If he agrees, I have no objection. As you know, here in Rome we also appreciate the 'romantic life.' An exclaustration would only be the final step."[27]

This cleared the path for the construction of a Zen house near Tokyo.

During the Rohatsu Sesshin in December 1966, the sixty-eight-year-old sat outside in the snow for an hour every night without feeling the cold. For the first time, shouting "Mu" at the top of his voice really helped him to "cut off" his thoughts.

---

[26] Letter to Fr. Pedro Arrupe, Hiroshima, April 10, 1966 (unpublished).
[27] Letter of Fr. Arrupe to Fr. Enomiya-Lassalle, Rome, May 1, 1966 (unpublished).

7

Traveler Between
East and West

❧

At an age when others retire and settle down, Hugo Lassalle embarked on a new journey—not only spiritually through the practice of zazen but also literally. He spent the next two decades mainly on the road, traveling in the name of Zen.

It was a time of great renewal. The Second Vatican Council ended in the fall of 1965. It had set the stage for greater openness to other religions and cultures. This reflected the changing state of the world. The 1960s brought massive change in many ways: European colonial rule had collapsed. The former colonies became so-called "underdeveloped countries" because the industrialized nations served as the benchmark against which these countries were judged. This greatly accelerated the process of globalization, and the structural dependencies and differences between the rich countries of the North and the poor countries of the South became clearly apparent.

At the Asian Catechetical Study Week in Manila in April 1967, which Lassalle attended on his way from Japan to Germany, exactly those problems were discussed that still preoccupied the church at that time. The first was the question of the relationship between the affluent church and the gospel's call to poverty, a question that would later be addressed by liberation theology. The other was the question of the relationship between the Christian, or rather Roman Catholic, tradition and the cultural and spiritual traditions of Asia. Lassalle himself had chosen poverty following the example of Jesus as his way of life, not only as a member of a religious order but out of personal conviction. And the integration of Christianity into the tradition of Asia, and especially into the tradition of Japan, had been a matter of course for him since his arrival in Japan in 1929, despite all the obstacles he had to face.

In Germany, reconstruction was more or less complete. West Germany was once again one of the most important industrialized countries, but rapid technological progress had led to a "mental-sociological situation"[1] of alienation, in which spiritual imbalances were becoming increasingly common, resulting in psychological and physical suffering. With this diagnosis, he was invited by the group "Doctors and Pastoral Care" (Gemeinschaft "Arzt und Seelsorger") to a conference on "Western Therapy and Eastern Wisdom" at Schloss Elmau in Bavaria in May 1967. Some four hundred people attended to hear lectures on the psychology of C. G. Jung, Yoga, Zen, Ayurveda, Tibetan and Chinese medicine, and other topics. In addition to Karlfried Graf Dürckheim who presented his Initiatic Therapy and I. H. Schultz, the founder of autogenic training, Hugo Enomiya-Lassalle was also invited.

His lecture, "The Way to Enlightenment in Zen Buddhism and Christian Mysticism," summarized the path he had taken up to that point. The experience at the heart of Zen practice, he said, is "a purely mental activity and therefore separate from

---

[1] Wilhelm Bitter, "Über Meditation in der Psychotherapie," in *Meditation in Religion und Psychotherapie*, ed. Wilhelm Bitter, 2nd ed. (Klett, 1972), 8.

all conceptualization. It can take on a different form, color, or interpretation depending on the worldview of the person experiencing it."[2] For Christians and Buddhists, it is the same basic experience, interpreted either in a Buddhist or Christian sense, depending on how a person's subconscious is shaped by their particular life context.[3]

People were very interested: more than one hundred people attended his introduction to Zen practice. *The desire to meditate is very strong. All these people, or most of them, have come to this path in search of a solution to their religious problems and are not currently receptive to the Church or, in some cases, [. . .] to Christianity in general.*[4]

This conference marked the beginning of the meditation movement in Germany. At Lassalle's suggestion, Fritz Kroeger, who had invited Lassalle to give a lecture at the University of Frankfurt after the conference, founded the "Frankfurter Ring e.V.," which still exists today and is one of the largest associations of meditation groups in Germany.[5] In the fall of 1968, Lassalle was invited to give a Zen course at the Benedictine monastery in Niederalteich, the first of countless courses he gave in Germany until his death in 1990.

In the late 1960s, the diversification or fragmentation of industrial society into different sectors began to be felt. Functionality, a key concept since the 1950s, was no longer limited primarily to questions of design and aesthetics. The functionality of industry and economy determined social processes; at the same time, the avant-garde of the postwar generation

---

[2] Wilhelm Bitter, *Abendländische Therapie und* östliche *Weisheit* (Klett, 1968), 115.

[3] *Cf.* Steven T. Katz, ed., *Mysticism and Religious Traditions* (Oxford University Press, 1983).

[4] May 5, 1967.

[5] Gerhard Wehr, *Karlfried Graf Dürckheim: Ein Leben im Zeichen der Wandlung* (Kösel, 1988), 264.

developed a sense of existential meaninglessness. The youth culture that emerged in the 1950s articulated this attitude in various ways.

By the end of the 1960s, people were searching for new ways of living; many young people became involved in Marxist groups and alternative communes, traveled to Asia, and embarked on psychedelic journeys of self-discovery—all attempts to escape the norms and order of industrial society's utilitarian rationality, its "symbolic universe" and its construction of reality.

Many at the time felt that humanity was on the verge of entering new spiritual dimensions. Some spoke of the dawn of the Age of Aquarius, others of a "mutation of humanity,"[6] and the Swiss cultural anthropologist Jean Gebser, whom Lassalle had met at Schloss Elmau, diagnosed a transformation of consciousness. Gebser drew on art and cultural history to show that such shifts in consciousness had occurred many times in the past, from magical to mythical and then to rational consciousness, and that we were now on the threshold of the transition to an arational or aperspectival consciousness.[7] The encounter between Asian and European cultures was the catalyst for this development. For Lassalle, Gebser's reflections confirmed his belief that Zen practice could contribute greatly to the spiritual development of humanity.

He had already written something similar in 1958 in an unpublished epilogue to his first book *Zen—Way to Enlightenment*. And some things seemed to point to new developments. The old structures of society began to crumble. Within just five years, between 1968 and 1973, the number of people attending

---

[6] Title of a book by Pierre Bertaux, Hölderlin researcher (originally published in French as *La mutation humaine*).

[7] Jean Gebser, *Ursprung und Gegenwart*, 3 vols. (Deutsche Verlags-Anstalt, 1949).

Sunday church services in Germany fell by a third[8]; ideological camps and Christian denominations as clearly defined social entities began to shift toward pluralism.

Interest in Asian religions was no longer confined to a narrow circle of academics, not least thanks to the Beatles and other icons of pop culture. When Lassalle gave a lecture on Zen, the hall was overflowing; it was not uncommon for there to be five hundred or more listeners, sometimes even a thousand. Lassalle spoke very simply and rather reservedly about Zen and the effects of zazen. The most important thing for him was to lead the people who had come to the lecture to sit down and sit quietly with them for a while. The lectures usually followed a similar pattern: "A tall, slender gentleman came to the lectern. After a few introductory words, he showed us how to sit, swung onto the table, crossed his legs, sat quietly—meditated—and so did we, for silence was the meditation."[9]

In August 1967, Lassalle flew back to Japan with a stopover in India. The Christian ashrams founded by the Benedictine Fathers Monchanin, Le Saux, and Griffiths were flourishing in their experiential dialogue between Christianity and Asian traditions. This time, Lassalle felt at home in India. At the Kurisumala Ashram on the west coast of India, led by Bede Griffiths, people now lived in the traditional Indian way, sitting on the floor, eating with their hands from palm leaves, and living in huts made of palm straw. The Roman liturgy had been replaced by the Syrian-Malabar liturgy of the Saint Thomas Christians.

From Madras (today Chennai) on the east coast of India, Lassalle visited Swami Abhishiktananda at the Shantivanam Ashram on the banks of the Kaveri River. Henri Le Saux had

---

[8] Karl Gabriel, *Christentum zwischen Tradition und Postmoderne*, 6th ed. (Herder, 1998), 52ff.

[9] Kurt Brill, in Harald Riese, ed., *Er lebt, was er lehrt: Auf dem Zen-Weg mit Pater Hugo M. Enomiya-Lassalle* (Friedenshof Verlag, 1990), 59.

come to India in 1947 as a Christian seeking dialogue with Indian spirituality. As a *sanyasin*, a homeless monk, he had taken the name Abhishiktananda and immersed himself in the spirituality of the Upanishads. In conversations with him, Lassalle found new clues to *the experience of the absolute.* This experience is *a completely pure experience of the self, without any admixture,* Le Saux said. The "self" here is not the individual ego, and there is no "higher" self to be distinguished from God. When Lassalle *said that if a Christian does Zen meditation correctly, it is ipso facto Christian meditation,* Abhishiktananda agreed.[10]

Lassalle learned another facet of interreligious dialogue in Sri Lanka from the Jesuit Aloysius Pieris, who combined his dialogue with Buddhism with social engagement in the village development projects of the (Gandhian) Sarvodaya movement. Together with him, Lassalle visited the renowned elderly Theravada monk Nyanaponika Mahathera (1901–1994)—a native German, who had lived in Sri Lanka since 1936—and two German Buddhists. These Theravada Buddhists rejected any connection between Zen and Christianity. They did not follow Lassalle's reasoning that Christian mysticism and Zen were about the experience of the absolute. One reason was that they believed that the Zen tradition did not refer to the Pali Sutras, the oldest tradition of Buddha's teachings. The Pali Canon, they said, did not deal with the experience of unity with the absolute.

The next six months brought a series of changes in Lassalle's life. In March 1968, after thirty years in Hiroshima, he moved to Tokyo. As a farewell gift, the mayor of Hiroshima, Yamada, made him an honorary citizen of Hiroshima. The two had known each other for forty years, as Lassalle had met Yamada during his studies in Oxford. Shortly thereafter, with

---

[10] August 16, 1967.

the support of his superiors, Lassalle was able to purchase a piece of land on the western outskirts of Tokyo, in the Akigawa Valley, near the small village of Koiwa, to build a new Zen retreat center, and he gained new confidence in his own prospects for satori. More and more requests for Zen courses came from Japan and Germany. With the permission of his superiors, Lassalle was allowed to use the income from his publications and courses to continue his Zen work.

Before Lassalle returned to Germany in August 1968, he told Sessui Roshi at Hosshinji about the Europeans' interest in Zen practice and their difficulty in adopting the lotus posture. The roshi said that Zen was for everyone, and that the lotus posture *was the best (ideal) posture for everyone. Zen therefore was not just a method. It was that, too, but it was everything, all of life, in every activity and every moment of rest; everything was Zen.*[11]

On August 24, 1968, three days after the Warsaw Pact troops had brutally put an end to the "Prague Spring" in Czechoslovakia, Lassalle's first Zen course in Germany began in the Benedictine monastery of Niederalteich near Passau. The participants were exhausted from the unfamiliar posture, even though the schedule of the Zen course was in no way comparable to the routine of a sesshin in a Zen monastery. This course was the first in a series that Lassalle gave primarily to clergy, but also to lay people. It soon became clear that *the faithful*, the lay people, were much more open to Zen practice than the clergy. Theologically trained priests and members of religious orders usually had difficulty with the fact that in Zen, there is neither a topic to contemplate nor an object to concentrate on. The objectless form of Zen meditation seemed, to many, to be a kind of rejection of the content of Christianity, even though objectless contemplation is part of Christian tradition.

---

[11] July 8, 1967.

On October 13, through the intervention of Father Arrupe and Cardinal Marella, Lassalle had an audience with Pope Paul VI. The Pope's blessing was very important to him. *The Pope asked what I was doing, and I replied, "Buddhism." The Pope immediately replied, "This is very important. We must find such things, such contacts. Thank you, I pray for you." Then I said, "I am particularly interested in Zen meditation." He asked if it was some kind of concentration. He also said that I had probably written books about it, which I confirmed.* Lassalle gave the Pope photos of Hiroshima and an invitation from the city of Hiroshima; he later sent him a copy of "Zen Buddhism" from Japan; Secretary of State Benelli replied that the Pope had read the book and gave it his apostolic blessing.[12]

In December 1968, the "Meeting of the Monastic Superiors of the Far East" was held in Bangkok. The theme was the question of what role Christian monks and nuns should play in the face of the political, social, and spiritual changes of the contemporary world. What value can a life of prayer and the search for selflessness have in a capitalist society? And what is the role of Christian monks and nuns in the cultural landscape of East Asia?

Lassalle was not only interested in the theme of the conference but, above all, in meeting Thomas Merton (1915–1968), the Trappist monk, writer, and staunch opponent of the Vietnam War. From Merton's book *The Ascent to Truth* (1951), Lassalle had learned that doubting acquired concepts of God is an important prerequisite for the path of mysticism. Merton illustrated this with the path of St. John of the Cross. Lassalle agreed with Merton's clear opposition to the Cold War and consumer society: this was a prerequisite for Christian mysticism and the realization of God. However, he had never corresponded with Merton and was, therefore, very interested

---

[12] Letter December 12, 1968 (unpublished).

in talking to him. After Merton's lecture on "Marxism and Monastic Perspectives"[13] the two had a brief opportunity to do so. Merton was tired. "We must talk at length sometime in Japan," Merton said. But by the evening of that day, Merton was dead, having been electrocuted by a fan in his hotel bathroom under circumstances that remain unclear to this day.

During his stay in Germany, Lassalle had not noticed much of the student riots of 1968, but when he arrived in Tokyo, conditions were akin to civil war in some areas. Students fought street battles with the police, which ended with the closure of Sophia University and other universities for six months and the arrest of the leaders. Lassalle was deeply shaken by the shouting and the police sirens, and when he held his annual retreat in the Jesuit residence on the campus of Sophia University, any noise that reminded him of this unsettled him. He felt tired and exhausted, in part because the fulfillment he longed for through satori had not come. The seventy-one-year-old wrote in his diary: *Lord Jesus, have mercy on me. And let everything else take its course. How much longer in this solitude and aridity* [. . .]. *And in the distance, I see eternity coming closer and closer. Living in intimacy with eternity.*[14] And then there were the everyday problems: *how to cope with not being able to finish,*[15] the never-ending tasks. And his everyday difficulties, such as *fear of people, depression, social withdrawal, insecurity, impatience, sensuality,* which could not simply be turned off but could only be dealt with by counterstrategies—for example, remaining silent when he became impatient, and trusting in God when depression overcame him. To keep going, *I can only find the strength to do this in union with Christ in God.*[16]

---

[13] Thomas Merton, *The Asian Journal of Thomas Merton,* ed. Patrick Hart, James Laughlin, and Naomi Burton Stone (New Directions, 1975).
[14] January 8, 1969.
[15] January 3, 1969.
[16] January 8, 1969.

On Holy Saturday, 1969, Lassalle signed the construction contracts for the Zen retreat center in the mountains west of Tokyo. By the end of May, the foundation posts of the wooden structure were in place, and the builders erected a small ridge-pole tree for the local Shinto gods. However, there were repeated difficulties with the Jesuit provincial, so Lassalle considered handing *the project* over to the Buddhists or a Christian order such as the Benedictines or Trappists, if there were continued difficulties with the Jesuits. Lassalle had become a sought-after spiritual mentor for members of religious orders; the Trappists in Hokkaido invited him to give a zazen retreat, as did the Benedictines in Korea. He took the opportunity to visit the famous Buddhist library from the thirteenth century at Haeinsa Monastery and also visited other Son monasteries (Son is the Korean pronunciation of Chinese "Ch'an" and Japanese "Zen"). He also met the highest-ranking Buddhist monk in South Korea, Suk Chung Dam, who said, *All religions should become one religion. He said that enlightenment was necessary and that once it was achieved, one would realize God.*[17]

Sessui Roshi, who had succeeded Lassalle's first teacher, Harada Roshi, at Hosshinji and who, like Harada Roshi, had given koans to his students, had died. His successor abandoned the practice of koans and emphasized, as was customary in Soto-shu, *shikantaza*, "just sitting." Lassalle did not cope well with this development. *One has no real basis for full commitment.*[18] So he began to search more intensively for a new Zen master.

Whatever he did in the world of fleeting appearances—*sabetsu no sekai* (the world of discriminations, the everyday world)—he did not feel happy; only when he was in *byodo no*

[17] April 21, 1969.
[18] March 3, 1969.

sekai (the world of nondiscrimination, emptiness) did he feel fulfilled. *I move between two worlds*,[19] he wrote. He experienced this state as deeply painful but also as a path of *purification of will* and spirit *through divine love*, as a form of the "night of the senses" described by the Spanish mystic John of the Cross. *The realization of one's own imperfection is probably not as complete in Zen as it is in this night of the senses.*[20]

Fr. Enomiya-Lassalle with Nagaya Roshi (1895–1993) in front of "The House of Tranquillity" (Haus der Stille) in Roseburg, Germany. Nagaya Roshi was one of the defining Zen teachers in Germany until 1990.

In August 1969, Lassalle traveled to Germany again, to the Buddhist House of Tranquility ("Haus der Stille") in Roseburg near Hamburg to give a Zen retreat. This was Lassalle's first contact with the German "meditation scene." Many of the participants in the ten-day sesshin had attended Satipatthana courses with a German Buddhist monk. Lassalle celebrated the Eucharist daily in the nearby parish church, and some of the group went to Mass with him, even though they were not Christians. Among them was Karin Stegemann, an elderly woman who had practiced meditation for many years in India and elsewhere. "Theoretically, and from my religious path, all this was very foreign to me. But since I had no res-

---

[19] June 1, 1969.
[20] March 3, 1969.

ervations about Father Lassalle and was completely open, I experienced how a higher power worked through him, which shook us all and had a deeply cleansing effect,"[21] she recalled. Celebrating the Eucharist with Father Lassalle was something special precisely because he did little more than read the prescribed texts in prayer, and for many people who came into contact with him, these were lasting experiences.

Lassalle did not actively seek dialogue with German Buddhists, but he was repeatedly invited to give lectures. "Eastern Meditation—A Remedy for the Western World" was the title of one of his lectures. For him, the practice of Zen pointed to a new global culture precisely because it was a form of objectless meditation. His encounters with Western Buddhists reinforced his perception of the situation of the church: *Catholics lack meditation.* [. . .] *Buddhists, on the other hand, have meditation in various forms; therefore, for some people, Catholicism is superseded by Buddhism, and they find peace there. They attain the ultimate, God.* So, it would be a great benefit to the church if meditation could be introduced into the church. *There is a tragedy in all this: those who convert to Buddhism eventually discover to their astonishment that what they admired in Buddhism is also present in Christian mysticism.*[22]

In a way, this corresponded to the otherwise much more radical view of his old philosophy teacher in Valkenburg and former superior, Father Wilhelm Klein (1889–1996), who Lassalle visited in Bonn, where he was working for the journal *Katholische Mission.* Klein believed that mission in the sense of Christianization was superfluous. If *the relationship between God and man* were embodied, then faith, hope, and love would already be present, and that was what mattered.

Through his lectures, Lassalle came into contact with all

[21] Karin Stegemann, in Riese, *Er lebt, was er lehrt,* 94.
[22] August 11, 1969.

kinds of people. Once, for example, a young blonde woman approached Lassalle. In 1952, Barbara Rotraut Pleyer had suddenly taken the microphone at the Olympic Games in Helsinki and called for an end to the Cold War. The newspapers had called her the "Angel of Peace of Helsinki." Now she was trying to organize a conference in Florence on "The Contribution of Religions to World Peace." During preliminary discussions for the conference, Lassalle met with physicists and Nobel Prize winners Werner Heisenberg and Carl Friedrich von Weizsäcker, as well as Swami Chidananda, one of India's most important spiritual figures at the time. The idea was to bring together scientists and people with spiritual experience to exchange ideas. At the conference in Florence, which finally took place in the fall of 1970 after many obstacles, one of the speakers was the Indian pandit Gopi Krishna. Through meditation, he had spontaneously entered extraordinary states of consciousness, which he recorded in a report entitled "The Biological Foundations of Religious Experience." C. F. Weizsäcker wrote a foreword to his book *Kundalini—Path to Higher Consciousness*, dealing with the connection between physiology and spirituality. For a long time, this little book was one of the most widely read works among people interested in meditation.

Queen Frederica of Greece (1917–1981) was interested in meditation, too. At the time, she was living in exile in Rome with her family and admired Lassalle's work. She gave him a gold cross for the tabernacle of the chapel in Shinmeikutsu. On his way to India in the winter of 1970, Lassalle stayed with her in Rome. She recommended that he visit Professor Mahadevan (1911–1983), an important Hindu scholar who taught philosophy at the University of Madras (today Chennai).[23] Lassalle did

---

[23] Telliyavaram Mahadevan Ponnambalam Mahadevan, *A Philosopher Looks Back* (Bharatiya Vidya Bhavan, 1982). Mahadevan reports also in detail about his encounter with Queen Frederica.

so and had a long conversation with him about the relationship between "sudden enlightenment" and "gradual cultivation." He also visited the ashram in Shantivanam again, where several people now lived in small palm-thatched huts. He then traveled via Calcutta (today Kolkata) to Bodh Gaya, where, according to tradition, the Buddha attained enlightenment. From there, he traveled to Darjeeling, where he introduced Zen to the local Jesuits and conversed with a Tibetan monk about meditation with and without an object. He then flew to Bangkok and traveled further south to Thailand to visit the highly respected yet controversial Theravada monk Buddhadasa (1906–1993) at Wat Suan Mokkh. Buddhadasa had set up a small museum in the monastery, which still exists today. In it, religious symbols of all religions can be seen, including a cross. Buddhadasa explained: *Everything comes down to destroying the ego. The cross is also a Buddhist symbol, as the vertical beam represents the ego, and the horizontal beam cuts through it. There is also a linden leaf.*

Buddhadasa believed that the only thing that mattered was realizing the realm of the absolute and that this did not require leaving one's own religion. Lassalle did not fully grasp this concept and wrote in his diary: *The monk wants to bring all religions together into one.*[24]

In mid-December, the Akigawa-Shinmeikutsu Zen retreat house was completed. The elongated building, which is set on stilts to protect it from possible flooding and has a shiny slate roof, is located on a small natural rock plateau below a narrow mountain road and above the Akigawa River, also known as the Autumn River. In the subtropical summer, the shade keeps the house pleasantly cool, but in winter, it is freezing cold. Lassalle moved there from Tokyo on December 16, and on December 19, the Archbishop of Tokyo, Shiranagi, consecrated the house.

---

[24] November 19, 1968.

Sixty people attended the opening, including some of Lassalle's Zen friends: Ban Roshi and Nishiwaki Roshi, for example. Lassalle celebrated midnight Mass on Christmas Eve with two women from the village. *The ladies from Tokyo cancelled at the last minute by telegram.*

Fr. Enomiya-Lassalle saying Mass in the chapel of Shinmeikutsu, the Zen Retreat House he built near Tokyo, together with Fr. Konno, SJ. The chapel is in Japanese style—a tatami room, a large rock serving as an altar, and another, larger, as tabernacle.

The first sesshin began at the end of March 1971. The participants were a mix of Japanese, European, and American, some Buddhists and most Christians or former Christians. A young Japanese Catholic named Some Masanori, who had been a monk in a Rinzai Zen monastery for some time, assisted Lassalle and ensured that everything ran as usual in a Zen monastery.

Media interest was high, and soon visitors began arriving from all over the world. There were Indians who had heard about Lassalle in India and were visiting Japan, German visitors to the EXPO, and American students. Even German President Gustav Heinemann (1899–1976) was interested in Lassalle.

The renowned physicist and philosopher Carl Friedrich von Weizsäcker (1912–2007) visited him, as did many other less famous people, all of whom were drawn to the remote place in the mountains west of Tokyo.

Lassalle felt that his personal journey had been far less successful than his external development. He felt that his Zen practice had not taken him far enough. The mystical experience he had had as a young man at the beginning of his studies in Valkenburg—*at that time, I called it the call of the cuckoo*—had been *a deeper and sweeter comfort.*[25] However, the deep longing for God that became increasingly clear in Zen practice motivated him to continue practicing. He realized that satori and mystical experience were closely related, yet he felt far removed from both. *I am one of those people who must continue wandering further and deeper into this labyrinth, perhaps never reaching the point where the light flashes—perhaps just a moment before death. Nevertheless, I must continue on the same path with complete dedication.* In such moments, his life seemed wasted. Such moods would disappear, but he had *to accept one as well as the other as they came.*[26]

Additionally, Lassalle became more of a public figure. For example, the Japanese television station NHK reported on the New Year's sesshin in Shinmeikutsu. However, since he had no "recognized" satori, he was vulnerable to his fellow Jesuits, which was often painful for him. He tried to accept it silently. Neither his fellow brothers nor the participants in the sesshins noticed the effort his path cost him. *I find it all a great burden, even though it has been so well received. I always have to fight and force myself to keep going. I try to calm myself with coffee and sweets, but that doesn't help much.* On the other hand, he saw that the people who came to the sesshins *gained a lot from*

---

[25] June 4, 1970.
[26] May 6, 1970.

them. [. . .] I have hardly found any exceptions. If that is the
case, then it is all worthwhile, even if I don't benefit from it. In
fact, it would be even more selfless.[27]

At Shinmeikutsu, sesshins took place every two months, even in the winter when the temperature was around or below freezing and the house had no heating. In between, Lassalle taught at Elisabeth University in Hiroshima and traveled frequently to teach Zen courses. He took advantage of these trips to learn more about the spiritual practices of other traditions, such as those in Korean Son monasteries. These practices differed significantly from those in Japanese Zen monasteries. In Korea, great importance was placed on studying Buddhist sacred texts, and monks and nuns could only participate in sesshins after five years of study. Sesshins took place twice a year and lasted three months rather than just a week or so, as was the case in Japan. Lassalle was impressed by the strict practice. "Afterwards, you don't know whether you are male or female," he would often joke in his lectures in Europe when talking about the Son monasteries.

However, the issues surrounding the integration of Zen were by no means over. Although the Second Vatican Council recommended integrating non-Christian values in its document *Lumen Gentium* § 17 and *Nostra Aetate* § 2, and international conferences encouraged theologians to become familiar with Asian religions, the superiors of the Japanese province only wanted to allow Zen practice to priests who had a *strong will*, *were Catholic from birth*,[28] and were good theologians. As was often the case, Lassalle's first impulse was to leave the order. But he decided to stay and work toward establishing a Catholic Zen monastery in Shinmeikutsu.

In the early 1970s, Zen had become a popular trend in Ger-

---

[27] January 1, 1971.
[28] April 20, 1971.

many, especially among young people. Even *Spiegel* magazine ran a cover story on the Zen boom.[29] Dürckheim and Lassalle were not the only ones teaching Zen in Europe. Since 1967, Nagaya Kiichi Roshi, a Tokyo-based philosophy professor, had been leading sesshins in Buddhist and Christian centers. In France, Deshimaru Taisen, a Soto school monk, began teaching around this time.[30]

When Lassalle returned to Germany in the fall of 1971, his courses and lectures were completely overcrowded. Many young people came to the events equipped with blankets and meditation cushions. The lectures always followed a similar pattern. The lean man in the shabby black suit gave a lengthy introduction to Zen practice for Christians. Then he took off his shoes, sat down on a table, and crossed one of his long legs over the other with astonishing agility, demonstrating the zazen posture. He invited people to sit with him, joined his fingers in mudra—a classic meditation gesture—and sat there breathing inaudibly, silently. A quietness emanated from him and enveloped those in the hall. Although he often seemed a little awkward, his simplicity and authenticity attracted people. Somehow, many felt a kind of "transformative power"[31] emanating from him.

Fascinated by India and Indian spirituality, Lassalle took every opportunity to learn more about them. For example, during a chance meeting in Cologne, he discussed meditation methods with the Hindu monk Sri Poonjaji (1910–1997), a disciple of Ramana Maharshi. *He has a method similar to Zen, there is no object. But the self must be found: Koan comes from KO AHAM, meaning who am I?*[32] Although there is no evi-

---

[29] Martin Baumann, *Deutsche Buddhisten: Geschichte und Gemeinschaften* (Diagonal, 1993), 80–82.

[30] Taisen Deshimaru, T., *Autobiographie eines Zen-Mönchs* (Theseus, 1986).

[31] Riese, *Er lebt, was er lehrt,* 96.

[32] October 30, 1971.

dence for this etymology in religious history, Lassalle retained it because it seemed meaningful to him. When you look closely at spiritual practices, they all ultimately boil down to answering this question: Who am I?

Lassalle traveled via Holland and Paris to Italy, giving courses and visiting acquaintances everywhere he went. He then made his way back to Japan via South India. Together with Professor Mahadevan from the University of Madras, Lassalle traveled to Kanchipuram to visit the Shankaracharya of Kanchi, one of the most important figures in the Hindu tradition and received *darshan*. From there, Lassalle traveled to Tiruvannamalai to visit Ramana Maharshi's ashram. Although the greatest Hindu saint (1879–1950) of the twentieth century had died twenty years earlier, the ashram still thrived through his presence. Lassalle sat down to meditate in the room where Ramana Maharshi had given *darshan*. He *had the thought that Ramana Maharshi was undoubtedly in heaven, a saint, and that one could ask for his intercession*[33]—for Shinmeikutsu and his own path.

Lassalle's next stop in South India was Pondicherry. He wanted to take a closer look at the spiritual experiment that is the city of Auroville. Auroville was founded as an ashram around Aurobindo Ghose (1872–1950). Ghose was a Bengali who discovered the Indian tradition while studying in England. He was initially imprisoned as a militant fighter for an independent India and had profound spiritual experiences in prison.

Together with his partner, Mira Alfassa (1878–1973), also known as "The Mother," a French-speaking woman of Turkish–Egyptian origin, he founded an ashram near Pondicherry intended to serve as the vanguard of a future spiritual evolution of humanity. Auroville in the 1970s was a small town with workshops, bakeries, farms, a university, hotels, and so

---

[33] December 13, 1971.

on. Everything done here was supposed to be karma yoga; all everyday activities were to be performed as spiritual practices so the entire community would live from the "supramental consciousness."

Lassalle stayed with the Catholic priest of Pondicherry and went to "The Mother" for *darshan* the next morning. Each visitor brought a small gift, and she placed her hand on each person's head in blessing. *When it was my turn, I watched the ritual and bowed my head slightly. However, she made no attempt to bless me. Instead, she smiled kindly, and I did the same.*[34]

Aurobindo, like Teilhard de Chardin, saw the spiritualization of matter as the next step in evolution. For this reason, the dogma of the bodily Assumption of Mary in 1950 was welcomed as an imminent evolutionary development of humanity. Satprem (Bernhard Enginger 1923–2007), one of the leading figures in Auroville alongside "The Mother," had just published a book, *The Mind of the Cells,* which described evolution as the spiritualization of matter. Hugo Lassalle also paid him a visit. *He had exceptionally accepted my visit, although he usually rejects everyone. He is completely imbued with the new era that is now dawning. All existing forms must disappear. This transition would be more significant than the transition from ape to human.*[35] The experience of the unity of opposites, previously the privilege of a few mystics, would then become accessible to many. From this experience, peace among humanity would finally emerge. Lassalle found this vision appealing because the image humans have of themselves determines their development.

Lassalle had been preoccupied with the phenomenology of spiritual experience for quite some time. In the writings of Ger-

[34] December 16, 1971.
[35] December 20, 1971.

man physician and philosopher Carl Albrecht (1902–1965), who studied with Karl Jaspers, Lassalle found a description that captured the complexity of the process. Albrecht describes the gradual de-imaging of the mind and the simultaneous process of integration in nonreligious language. This process can be found in both Christian mysticism and Zen. One of Japan's most important Zen masters, Irie Hayashi, abbot of Tofukuji in Kyoto, confirmed this as well—contrary to the usual reticence of Zen monks when it comes to experiences on the Zen path.[36]

Lassalle's book, *Meditation as a Path to the Experience of God: A Guide to Mystical Prayer,* published in 1972 (in German as *Meditation als Weg zur Gotteserfahrung: Eine Anleitung zum mystischen Gebet*), provided a clear and readable summary of Carl Albrecht's observations during mystical experiences, linking them to Christian mysticism and Zen.

The general public increasingly recognized Lassalle's work to integrate Zen practice into Christianity. This resulted in a huge volume of mail, which he answered himself. A team from the Pontifical Mission Society in Vienna made a film about Shinmeikutsu, the "Cave of Divine Darkness." The first long-term guests from Germany arrived at the retreat house in the mountains west of Tokyo. Forty or more people registered for the sesshins in Shinmeikutsu. Lassalle was also invited by non-Christian institutions in Japan to lead sesshins. Most notably, he and a second priest were chosen to be instructors in inculturation and mentors to four young Jesuits in Shinmeikutsu.

In July 1972, he suddenly suffered a bout of paralysis during his afternoon nap. At first, he thought he was dying, yet

---

[36] Verbal communication from Hans Fischer-Barnicol. Albrecht's phenomenological descriptions apply not only to Christian spirituality but also to Zen practice. This was discovered by Hans Fischer-Barnicol, Carl Albrecht's estate administrator, during a nine-month stay at Tofukuji. Irie Hayashi, the abbot of the monastery and an important Zen master, confirmed Albrecht's steps and descriptions on this occasion.

he did not fear death. Something seemed to be changing. A month later, during the August sesshin in Shinmeikutsu, he read an excerpt from a book by Karl Rahner, the eminent German Jesuit: *The experience of eternity, the experience that the spirit is more than a part of this temporal world, the experience of risk and leap of faith [. . .]: the experience of God.*[37] After the sesshin, he took the bus from Koiwa down the winding road to the local train station to Tokyo. He looked out at the densely wooded mountain slopes. *At that moment, I felt a desire to become one with everything. For the first time, I understood the Eastern notion that everything returns to and is reunited with the one. Before, I had found it inconceivable that anyone could feel happy about the thought of losing their individual personality. Now, I had no resistance to it whatsoever. This does not mean that I believe in the dissolution of the human person.*[38]

Lassalle had been searching for a new Zen master for some time—more precisely, since the death of Sessui Roshi, Harada's immediate successor—but had not yet found a suitable candidate. The sesshin with Yasutani Roshi, one of Harada's successors, irritated him with its warlike ferocity. He did not want to go to the Zen nunnery Kannonji either. While speaking with Elaine McInnes (1924–2022), a Canadian Catholic nun who had taught at the Elisabeth Music Academy in Hiroshima for many years alongside Lassalle, he repeatedly heard about Yamada Koun Roshi in Kamakura. Since Yamada Koun Roshi welcomed Christians to his zendo, Lassalle decided to send the four young Jesuits he was mentoring there for the December 1972 Rohatsu Sesshin and to participate himself.

---

[37] August 28, 1972. The quote is from: Karl Rahner, "Über das Beten," in *Geist und Leben* (March–April 1972): 91.
[38] August 27, 1972.

Unlike Harada Roshi and Yasutani Roshi, Yamada Koun Roshi was a layman. Born in 1907, he was nine years younger than Lassalle, who was seventy-four at the time. He worked as a manager and had three adult children. Yamada began practicing Zen during the war in Manchuria under the influence of his friend, the Zen monk Nakagawa Soen (1907–1984), who later became a roshi. After the war, Yamada lived in Kamakura, an old temple town on the outskirts of Tokyo, and became a student of Yasutani Roshi. One evening, on his way home from work, he read the

Yamada Koun Roshi (1905–1989) in the San'un-Zendo, Kamakura.

famous words of Zen master Dogen on the train: "Mind is nothing but mountains, rivers, and the great earth; nothing but the sun, the moon, and the stars."[39] In the middle of the night, he awoke with these words in his mind. Overcome with immense joy, he burst into loud, almost inhuman laughter, waking his family and neighbors. The next morning, Yasutani Roshi confirmed in dokusan that Yamada had experienced an unusually deep awakening and kensho. In 1967, Yasutani appointed him a Zen master. In 1970, Yamada Roshi became the head of the Sanbokyodan, a lay Zen association founded by Yasutani in 1954. Following the tradition of Harada Roshi, Yasutani—who was originally a Soto Zen priest—sought to combine the best

---

[39] Kazuaki Tanahashi, ed., *Moon in a Dewdrop. Writings of Zen Master Dōgen* (Farrar, Straus and Giroux, 1985), 88f.

of Soto and Rinzai Zen. Neither the elaborate daily rituals of monasteries nor the study of sutras, the sacred texts, were considered important in the Sanbokyodan because the decisive factor is seen in awakening, that is, kensho.[40]

Like many Japanese people, Yamada Koun attended catechism classes after the war. He sent his sons to Jesuit schools and had repeated contact with Christianity during his extended stays in the US. For him, the connection between Zen Buddhism and Christianity was embodied in the phrase, "The kingdom of God is within you" (Luke 17:21).[41] Since the late sixties, Christians had been practicing Zen in his zendo; the first was the Jesuit Thomas Hand (1920–2005) in 1969.

The zendo, located on a side street in Kamakura, was part of the Yamada family home. During sesshin, around forty people, including about ten Japanese and Western Christians, slept and sat in the seventy-square-meter space. The koan "Mu" was neither shouted forcefully nor pushed into the body with the breath. Yamada Roshi, who spoke English well, explained to Lassalle in dokusan that he should follow his breath with "Mu." Through his conversations with Yamada Roshi, Lassalle realized that becoming a Zen master himself was a distant prospect. The koan "Mu" was only the beginning. According to the Sanbokyodan order, one must solve around six hundred more koans before being awarded the title of Zen teacher.

During this sesshin, the roshi recognized the kensho of Sister Elaine McInnes and Sister Alexander from the Carmelite monastery near Osaka, where Lassalle had been teaching Zen

---

[40] Robert H. Sharf, "Sanbōkyōdan: Zen and the Way of the New Religions," *Japanese Journal of Religious Studies* 22, no. 3/4 (Fall 1995): 417–58.

[41] During the first meeting between Father Enomiya-Lassalle and Yamada Koun Roshi, the latter recounted that he had heard the words "The kingdom of God is within me" for the first time in America, and that this was where Christianity and Buddhism could meet. He was very surprised, because Christians usually pray "Our Father who art in heaven." Christianity was outward-looking, while Bukkyo was inward-looking. (December 11, 1963).

for years. Both had come to Zen through Lassalle, and he felt a little like Moses, who leads the others to the Promised Land but then dies without reaching it himself. *I lead others to the Promised Land, but I myself never enter it. That is just my task.*[42]

In Hugo Lassalle's life, however, there was another dimension to his experience besides the pursuit of enlightenment. As with most things very close to him, he did not write much about this dimension in his diaries. The secret of his life was the experience of Christ's presence. From this presence came the strength for discipleship and the willingness to accept the suffering that comes with life. It also gave him the ability to die a little more to his own selfishness each day. *I am not oriented toward suffering but toward freedom from it. It would have to be like the officer said in Hiroshima when he left for war: Not until we meet again—but I am leaving to die [. . .]. That is depressing. But without it, I cannot find peace.*[43] He practiced this dying in many small steps of asceticism, beginning with quitting smoking in 1949 to better progress on the spiritual path and ending with his *acts of penance.* The penitential belt found among his belongings—a piece of scratchy fabric worn on bare skin—was well-worn and clearly well-used. Lassalle knew that this was a sign of a past spirituality that might not continue into the future. *This may be a sign that I am backward in light of the "new man." However, everyone must do what is right for them at the right time and not take any leaps.*[44]

During these years, Lassalle lost two people who were close to him. In the spring of 1972, Fukuhara Eigan, the monk from Kokutaiji, passed away. He encouraged Lassalle in many conversations about his Zen path, repeatedly pointing him toward the classical Chinese Zen tradition and criticizing Japanese

---

[42] February 17, 1973.
[43] February 17, 1973.
[44] February 8, 1973.

Zen institutions. The following year, in March 1973, Father Goossens, who was very close to Lassalle, passed away. His death shook Lassalle as much as the death of his older brother, Bernhard, in World War I, and this time, he did not hold back his tears. They flowed for four days, no matter how hard he tried not to show it.

The major obstacle on Father Lassalle's Zen path was the philosophical and theological training received during his studies, as well as the training of his intellect and will during decades of annual retreats. Schooled in neo-scholastic thinking, Lassalle considered "Mu" to be a metaphysical expression. But that was beginning to change. On Pentecost Sunday, Lassalle noted, *Now Mu and God are exactly in line; they have become one. Mu is everything.*[45] The change was also noticeable to outsiders. Lassalle's fellow Jesuit, Father Kadowaki, who was studying Zen under Yamada Koun at the time, attended one of Lassalle's lectures and approached the roshi afterward: "Father Enomiya could not speak about Zen in this way if he had not attained kensho."[46] Kadowaki, a fellow Jesuit who had studied theology, also told the roshi that Lassalle's training in scholastic philosophy hindered his understanding of Buddhist terminology. It was not until after the Rohatsu Sesshin in December 1972, that is, about a decade and a half after he began serious Zen practice, that he understood that the terms "Mu" and "Buddha nature" both refer to the absolute. This notion is based on around a thousand years of Buddhist philosophy, during which time the "absolute reality" of awakening has been reflected upon and interpreted by various schools. These reflections have impacted the respective forms of practice.

Yamada Roshi took up Kadowaki's point. On the penulti-

---

[45] June 10, 1973.
[46] Enomiya-Lassalle, Kensho-Report, September 7, 1973 (unpublished manuscript).

mate day of the sesshin, he told Lassalle in dokusan that *he believed I had understood. But that I had developed a certain concept of kensho [. . .] under the influence of philosophy [. . .]. Since it did not occur, I thought that I had no kensho. Then, he explained that my kensho could have been a Christian kensho, something like an experience of God. But that was also kensho. Since he had often had Catholic priests or clergy as students, he had already considered this possibility.*[47]

Yamada Roshi then tested Father Lassalle in dokusan according to the Harada lineage's rules; he asked him, "What is Mu?" and explored this question in all its facets. This is not about intellectual understanding, but rather the student's "realization," or an instantaneous, embodied understanding of the one reality. While words are involved, it is primarily about "heart-to-heart" communication. Lassalle knew he wouldn't have been able to answer these questions during the Rohatsu sesshin in the winter. Afterward, Sister Elaine McInnes told him that she had experienced "Mu" in a cat's meow. This made Lassalle wonder if he had experienced something similar for years while driving his car, for example, or hearing. *It was only shortly before the sesshin that I realized I could describe my experiences while driving as muji-seeing or -hearing. It gradually dawned on me what muji actually was.* The shock of Father Goossens's death had also *undone something that had to be undone for kensho*, he reflected in his diary.[48]

At the end of the July sesshin in Kamakura, the roshi announced that Father Lassalle had attained kensho during the sesshin. *He criticized [. . .] the Japanese Zen masters and himself for being overly attached to form where kensho was concerned.*

[47] July 27, 1973.
[48] July 27, 1973.

On the last evening of the sesshin, with the roshi's permission, Lassalle celebrated Mass in his bedroom, together with the Catholic participants, including Kadowaki, Benedictine Abbot Odo Haas, and Sister Elaine McInnes. It was July 31, the holiday of St. Ignatius, founder of the Jesuits.

Within a few days, Lassalle's situation had changed dramatically. Filled with gratitude, he recalled his teachers: Shimada Roshi, with whom he did his first sesshin at Eimy-oji in Tsuwano in 1943; Watanabe Genshu Roshi; Harada Sogaku Roshi; Sessui Roshi, Harada's successor; Yasutani Roshi; and Nagasawa Roshi from Kannonji. They had all accompanied him on his journey. Nevertheless, he was perplexed by the sudden shift. He could not remember any "breakthrough" experience. *The recognition of a kensho from the past, which no one knew when, where, or how it had occurred, came as a complete surprise to me. I couldn't believe my ears, and it felt like I was dreaming.* Perhaps the simplest explanation is *a "gradual" enlightenment* [. . .], *although this theory is rejected by the masters. At least in the sense that the actual tipping point cannot be identified.* [. . .] *It is doubtful that a Christian religious experience underlies kensho, though I could cite such experiences from the past. I would not have attained kensho without the Christian experience. Many things likely contributed, especially the numerous*

sesshin and zazen [. . .] *over 30 years, particularly the last 17 years. The fruit ripened slowly and became ripe. However, it did not fall from the tree with great noise and emotion.*

The long-awaited "great liberation" mentioned so often in books had not occurred. *The result is that I must continue to struggle with the difficulties of my temperament until liberation is achieved.* The sesshin marked *the end of one period and the beginning of a new one.*[49] Once the koan Mu has been resolved, insight is deepened and refined through many more koans.

Beyond its individual significance for Father Lassalle, however, the sesshin also had a historical dimension. *At the end of the last dokusan, Roshi told me that he wanted to give Zen to Catholicism. That was his task. However, we would have to find out for ourselves how to integrate it there. He told everyone something similar.*[50]

The Zen tradition of "transmission outside the scriptures, from heart to heart" began to merge with the Christian tradition. Yamada Roshi believed that Zen would one day become important in the Catholic Church.[51]

---

[49] July 27, 1973.

[50] July 27, 1973.

[51] Robert Aitken, "Remembering Yamada Koun Roshi," *Eastern Buddhist* 23, no. 1 (Spring 1990): 152–54.

8

On the Horizon:
Openness, Void

❧

What is left when you take away the various theologies that have developed around the Gospels over the course of two thousand years? Who is Christ? What does it mean to be a Christian? These were questions that preoccupied Lassalle during the last two decades of his life. These questions were sharpened by the koan practice, which confronted Lassalle with a philosophical world completely different from the scholastic philosophy he had known until then. For someone like Lassalle, who had gone through the rigorous school of thought of neo-Scholasticism, koan practice was a great challenge. This is because neo-Scholasticism is based on a hierarchy of phenomena—that is, things, living beings, etc.—that are oriented toward the "Absolute," that is, God, and derives its meaning from this orientation. Koan practice, on the other hand, follows the Chinese Mahayana tradition, which holds that the "Absolute" is present in the concrete particular.

The classical philosophical proofs of God, which he had studied intensively in order to lead people to God, also stood in the way of his koan practice, since koan practice is not about concepts but about an embodied understanding and realization of the "absolute" here and now. In each koan, characters from the "Golden Age" of Zen appear as actors in scenes set in the monastic world of ancient China and marked by Buddhist philosophy. These short anecdotal sequences are like "precedents" for how the "ultimate reality," "the absolute" is present in the concrete here and now. The student then demonstrates his understanding of the koan in his encounter with the roshi. The "supermundane truth" beyond dualities and concepts is articulated in the "in-between" of teacher and student; this is the dimension of koan practice. In a sense, the world of the Bible is much closer to this world than the world of neo-scholastic philosophy, and so although Lassalle had difficulties with his neo-scholastic philosophical background, koan practice transformed and deepened his approach to the Gospel, which seemed to him to be increasingly *exhilarating.*[1]

Early on, during his first visit to Germany after the war in the fall of 1947, he had noticed that the philosophical explanation of God's existence through the classical proofs no longer moved people. And the more he concentrated on cultivating inner silence according to the instructions of *The Imitation of Christ*, the more God as a concept disappeared from his mind. This development began even before his intensive Zen practice, and it frightened him, but on the other hand, he thought, *We cannot limit God to our concepts. This is a comfort to me, because lately I have felt strongly the inconceivability of God.*[2] This made the person of Jesus even more important to him. Through the nonconceptual and objectless practice of Zen, he later developed a deeper understanding of people who turned away from traditional religions and toward atheism. *Atheism*

---

[1] November 20, 1976.
[2] February 24, 1957.

is partly a step forward in that man no longer comes to God through proofs or creatures but demands an experience of God,[3] he said during a conversation between Buddhists and Christians in Kyoto.

In Europe, interest in Zen was growing: Mimi Marechal (1937–1995), one of the most influential Catholic advocates of Zen in the Netherlands, came to Japan in 1973 to invite Lassalle to De Tiltenberg, a house run by "De Graal," ("The Grail") an ecumenical international women′s movement advocating for peace and social justice. Until 2003, De Tiltenberg was an important center for interfaith encounter, feminist theology, and Zen practice in the Netherlands. Around the same time, Emmanuel Jungclaussen (1927–2018), a Benedictine priest and later abbot in the monastery of Niederalteich and one of the most important spiritual writers in the German-speaking world, came to Kamakura for two months to visit Yamada Roshi. It was precisely through the practice of Zen that "a new

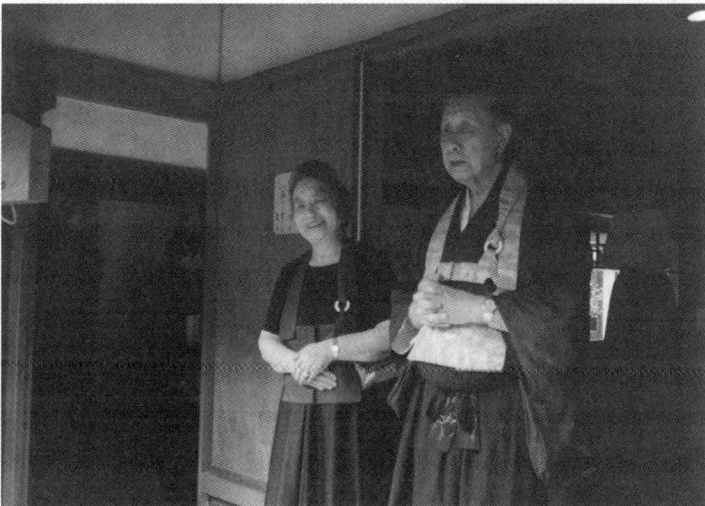

Yamada Koun Roshi and his wife, Dr. Kazue Yamada, who supported Fr. Lassalle's endeavor.

---

[3] August 27, 1973.

approach to the Jesus Prayer grew in him," he later wrote, so that this time in Kamakura, which Lassalle had arranged for him, became "the most important experience"[4] of his spiritual journey.

Lassalle could not forget India. In September 1973, he visited Bodh Gaya, the place where the Buddha had experienced his awakening, to meditate in this atmosphere under the Bodhi tree, supposedly a descendant of the tree under which the Buddha had sat. However, he found nothing special about it. On the other hand, he found the practice of Vipassana very helpful, which he practiced for several days under the guidance of the Burmese Theravada monk Anagarika Munindra (1915–2003), to whom the noted Vipassana teacher Joseph Goldstein and others refer. The increasingly subtle awareness of the flow of thoughts and intentions opened up a dimension not practiced in Zen. Perhaps this is why Lassalle later invited S. N. Goenka (1924–2013), another important Vipassana teacher, to give courses in Shinmeikutsu.

The next stop on the trip to India was the Shivananda Ashram in Rishikesh. Lassalle participated in the *arati*, the evening fire ceremony, and then Swami Satyananda invited him to speak about his spiritual path the next afternoon, that is, to give *satsang*. This honor was given to only a few visitors of the Shivananda Center. In the evening, he stood on the banks of the Ganges in Haridwar; people placed candles decorated with flowers on the water as floating prayers. The young Indian who accompanied Lassalle drew water from the river with his hand and drank it, and Lassalle followed suit. When he went to buy train tickets to Delhi—as usual for the cheapest third class, which was notoriously overcrowded—the swami appeared

---

[4] Emmanuel Jungclaussen, "Herzensgebet und Dreieinigkeit nach ostkirchlicher Überlieferung," *Die beiden Türme, Niederaltaicher Rundbrief* 33-1, no. 71 (1997): 34.

unexpectedly, and tickets were bought for Lassalle for the first-class air-conditioned sleeper car, the most expensive category. From there, he traveled across the Indian continent to Madras, from there to Auroville, the city of spiritual experimentation, and then back to Tiruvannamalai, the ashram of the late great saint Ramana Maharshi. He had achieved what Lassalle had tried to live: he *never demanded anything special for himself. First came the animals, then the poor and the lepers, then the guests, and finally, the members of the ashram and himself.*[5]

In between, Lassalle gave lectures on Zen and Christian mysticism to the young Jesuits in Kodaikanal in the Palani Mountains near Madurai; then, back in Chennai, he met Professor Mahadevan and Queen Frederica of Greece. With them, he traveled to Kanchipuram to visit the Shankaracharya of Kanchi, who, now nearly blind, had retired to a small hut. He *still had the same pure, kind smile as two years earlier but did not speak a word.*[6] When Queen Frederica said that she considered the Shankaracharya, Professor Mahadevan, and Lassalle to be great saints, Lassalle explained to her that *I am only a beginner and that she should definitely lower her high opinion of his experience.*[7] Later, he learned that the Acharya lived in a state of deep, blissful contemplation. *Afterward, I doubted that Japanese Zen masters ever reach this state.*[8]

Lassalle then took part in the Asian Monastic Meeting in Bangalore, together with the sinologist Yves Raguin, SJ (1912–1998), the theologian and philosopher Raimon Panikkar (1918–2010), and the Buddhist scholar Aloysius Pieris (1934–), all important voices in interreligious dialogue. In conversation with the Tibetan monks who attended the conference as representatives of the Dalai Lama, the question of a

---

[5] October 4, 1973.
[6] October 12, 1973.
[7] October 12, 1973.
[8] October 13, 1973.

personal God soon arose. For the Tibetans, a "personal God" was a person *who had reached the highest level of enlightenment through meditation and his life.* So "personal God" means something very different to these Tibetan monks than it does in the Christian tradition. A Japanese Benedictine nun tried to explain the Christian understanding to one of the Tibetans. "God" is much more like "ultimate reality," a term used in English translations of Buddhist texts for "the Absolute," "Buddha nature," and similar expressions. The Benedictine nun asked the Tibetan monk *if he believed that Absolute Reality loved him. He replied: Yes. The nun then said: This is what we mean by a personal God.*[9]

Although Lassalle was very satisfied with the conference, he felt that an essential dimension was missing: *We did not solve the problem of witnessing poverty.*[10] Lassalle hardly ever spoke about social issues or liberation theology, and many people who came to his meditation courses in Europe wanted nothing to do with such topics. But for Father Lassalle, social commitment was a natural part of his life, and he lived the poverty he had vowed as a member of a religious order in an exemplary way, without saying much about it. He was a man of few possessions; when he traveled, he carried a small black suitcase, and that was all. His suits and cassocks came from deceased brothers and were heavily patched, and this was how he traveled between Asia and Europe.

At the beginning of November 1973, Gunter Stachel organized a symposium on Zen practice in Mainz in honor of Lassalle's seventy-fifth birthday,[11] after which Lassalle received an honorary doctorate from Gutenberg University Mainz. Otherwise, there were no celebrations, partly because Lassalle did

---

[9] October 16, 1973.
[10] October 22, 1973.
[11] Report from the meeting, in Hugo M. Enomiya-Lassalle, *Zen-Meditation: Eine Einführung* (Benzinger, 1975).

not tell anyone that he was turning seventy-five. On November 11, he wrote in his diary: *75 years old! Ama nesciri [love of being unknown] came to my mind just in time, and I didn't 'report in.' I silently thanked God for everything.*

After stopovers in Vienna and Rome, Lassalle traveled to the German Democratic Republic, which was much easier for him as a Japanese citizen than it was for people from Western Germany. In Erfurt, he secretly held a Zen course, the first of a long series that ended even before 1989, the year in which the Berlin Wall fell.

In the mid-1970s, something like a meditation movement had emerged in Germany as a countermovement to the increasing rationalization of everyday life. Inner peace and revitalization were the themes around which the courses revolved. Within the church, the protagonists of the meditation movement—such as the well-known religious educator and liturgist Klemens Tilmann (1904–1984)—turned against moralism, formal piety, and empty theological formulas. Attempts were made to quickly train "meditation leaders" for work in parishes, who then taught a mixture of group-dynamic methods, meditative dance, and relaxation exercises such as eutony (a practice based on sensory awareness) and zazen. Lassalle found the discussions about the methods and their possible applications in "meditation leader courses" tedious and fruitless. He was not interested in short-term projects but in a consistent and fundamental transformation of life as a whole. His model was Jesus. That is why Lassalle was always interested in courses on "spiritual healing," because, following the example of Jesus, *"this is also part of it."* He considered incorporating the dimension of healing into dokusan.[12]

The courses he attended at Falshöft—at the center of the van Ogtrops, a couple practicing alternative healing methods—

---

[12] April 19, 1974.

focused on somatic awareness through eutonic and other exercises. Lassalle, who was seventy-six at the time, approached the exercises with great openness. *An inner glow developed that opened me up to others in a way I had never experienced before . . .* It was as if *a wall had come down. The result could be called a discovery of the feminine, which then gives rise to a corresponding need.*[13] But the decisive factor was *the feeling of inner warmth*, a sense of spiritual love that was familiar to him.

If one considers Zen and Christianity as embodied paths of practice, then they differ in the focus of attention, Lassalle reflected after these courses. In Zen, attention is focused on the hara, the area just below the navel, and this opens up a "cosmic dimension." The Prayer of the Heart or Jesus Prayer, on the other hand, directs the breath to the heart center. *Christian spirituality resides in the heart chakra* and is related to others. The two somatic centers are not mutually exclusive but rather interdependent. *Perhaps there is a progression from the cosmic to the personal? [. . .] These connections should be explored.*[14] In discussions with Western Buddhists (e.g., with Philip Kapleau) about Zen as a religion of salvation through "self-power" (*jiriki*) and Christianity as a religion of salvation through "other-power" (*tariki*), Lassalle was therefore always very reserved, due to these and other considerations.

He found it difficult to deal with people who came from the Christian charismatic "scene" and were angry about Zen courses in Catholic monasteries and educational institutions. *The devil would have to be exorcised from me, so to speak, apart from the fact that I don't even know if there is such a thing as a devil,*[15] Lassalle remarked. The prayer meetings of the charismatic reform movement, which he later attended in Tokyo,

---

[13] January 2, 1974.
[14] January 25, 1974.
[15] February 26, 1974.

seemed to him to emphasize the irrational. *In this way, the same phenomena did not occur in the early Church*, he observed. On the other hand, the usually reserved Japanese thawed out at this meeting, shaking hands and hugging each other. *From time to time, I would like to do that again*,[16] Lassalle thought, but the strongly dualistic element in it prevented him from doing so. In 1974, a visit between two sesshins in the ecumenical community of Taizé with Frère Roger Schutz, who was interested in the effect of Zen on prayer, made a deep impression on Lassalle: *Here in Taizé, the boundaries between Christian denominations have clearly disappeared.*[17] This pointed in a new direction, he thought.

When Lassalle was in Europe, he gave one Zen course after another, mostly in Germany and the Netherlands but also in France, Italy, and Austria. He used the few days off to visit an elderly cousin who lived in the Netherlands, also a nun, or his two sisters in Germany. A friend, a cancer specialist, had discovered a "growth" in his body, and Lassalle began the recommended therapy but had to abandon it for lack of time. On Holy Saturday in 1974, he flew to the US to give lectures on Zen in Zen Buddhist and Christian monasteries on the East and West Coasts. Back in Japan, his daily life was increasingly filled with Zen courses, which he taught himself, and weekends and sesshins in Kamakura with Yamada Roshi. Lassalle was to complete the Sanbokyodan koan training as quickly as possible, which would take about three years, the roshi had said. The goal of becoming a Zen teacher for Christians seemed within reach.

However, his efforts were hardly appreciated by the Jesuits at Sophia University, the community where Lassalle lived. Lassalle found confirmation of his path in the Zen group in

---

[16] May 18, 1975.
[17] January 13, 1974.

Kamakura, to which he felt very connected. Once again, he considered leaving the order, but he *rejected* this idea. He had decided to follow the path of Jesus. *I should, therefore, not seek respect, but rather contempt. That is the imitation of Christ.*[18] During his annual retreat in June 1974, he began preliminary work on a book on the relationship between the Ignatian Exercises and Zen. *As far as the method of meditation is concerned, zazen begins precisely where the Ignatian exercises end.* Since the days of Ignatius, however, the Catholic Church had changed a lot, not least because of the aggiornamento after the Second Vatican Council. *Zen, on the other hand, is hardly touched by today's intellectual world, even in Japan. The forms are rigid and inflexible, as if without them the thing itself would be lost or in grave danger.*[19] Some Japanese also felt this way. The philosophers of the Kyoto School, who took Zen Buddhism as the basis of their philosophy, spoke of the need for Zen to "shed its skin" in order to meet the demands of the present.[20] Together with the two heads of the school, Keiji Nishitani (1900–1990) and Shizuteru Ueda (1926–2019), Lassalle prepared a symposium for his friend Hans Fischer-Barnicol (1930–1999) in Kyoto in September 1974.

The Cistercians invited Lassalle to Vietnam to give introductory courses in Zen and sesshin. Here, too, he went in search of the Zen tradition and learned that there were few good Zen masters, since most practiced a kind of esoteric Zen—such as "out-of-body travel" and other esoteric abilities that are considered obstacles to enlightenment in Zen practice.

In March 1975, Lassalle began his annual retreat while also

---

[18] June 7, 1975.

[19] June 9, 1974.

[20] Kôichi Tsujimura, "Die Wahrheit des Seins und das absolute Nichts," in *Die Philosophie der Kyoto-Schule*, ed. Ryôsuke Ohashi (Verlag Karl Alber, 1990), 441–54.

giving retreats to young Jesuits preparing for ordination. He was quite depressed and longed to finally be able to live from God and become free within himself.

The following lines from the notes of the last day of these retreats are all underlined in Lassalle's diary; they are the only passages of this kind in the many diary notebooks from 1945 to 1990. *This morning, in the first meditation. One could say: one descends into the ground, or even more strongly: one is consumed by it (Ruysbroek). It is the divine ground.*

The Buddhist also goes this far. For Christians, on the other hand, the Logos is born from the ground, appears in Christ, and in him a new divine encounter takes place. An encounter from person to person. In this encounter, there is also the Holy Spirit, who is love.

It was not easy for him to return to everyday life after the profound experience of this retreat. *"Nothing to hope for and nothing to fear." Nothing happens without God's will or permission. This should be enough for me,*[21] he wrote in his diary.

The openness to new ideas and experimentation that had characterized the general climate since the mid-1960s began to give way to new boundaries and divisions in the mid-1970s. Western Zen Buddhists began to criticize Christians who practiced Zen. Zen was a traditional Buddhist practice, they argued, and Christians could not practice Zen and remain Christians. Christian theologians, in turn, began to view Zen with suspicion as an "objectless practice." They forgot that objectless meditation, called "contemplation," is an essential part of the Christian tradition. They feared that biblical revelation and the uniqueness of Christ would be relativized by the influence of Asian religions. "Meditation is betrayal,"[22] was the succinct

---

[21] March 13, 1975.

[22] Hans Urs von Balthasar, "Meditation als Verrat," *Geist und Leben* 50 (1977): 260–68 is the most pronounced position at that time and until today.

way in which the theologian and later Cardinal Hans Urs von Balthasar summed up the objections. Eastern meditation practices, he believed, were a "world-denying mysticism of unity," whereas Christianity, through the incarnation of Christ, made it possible to embrace creation. The fact that neither Buddhism nor Hinduism requires the denial of the world in order to experience the "absolute" and that it is not simply a matter of "unity" was simply overlooked.

Another argument that has been used repeatedly is that Zen lacks a personal God. This position was taken, for example, by the Jesuit Josef Sudbrack (1925–2010).[23] Lassalle argued that this would mean that God's mercy is limited if God *cannot help when people do not say "you" even though they do their best, or he does not want to help.*[24] It also seemed to him that the discussion ignored the experience of Christian mystics who testified to experiencing God as both personal and impersonal.

Despite all the polemics and reservations of the theologians, Lassalle's Zen courses were always overcrowded, and one had to register very early to get a place in the sesshin. Lassalle had adopted the basic, simple gestures of Zen practice from the elaborate ritual of Japanese Zen temples: sitting, walking, and bowing. All that remained of the concert of gongs, drums, and bells were the wooden blocks and the bell that marked the beginning and end of the sitting and walking periods. No sutras, bodhisattva precepts, or other texts were recited. The practice took place in concentrated silence. Once a day, a Eucharist was celebrated, which could be attended voluntarily by anyone. The room used as a zendo contained a candle and flowers and usually, but not always, a cross.

The theological problem that moved Lassalle most deeply

---

[23] Josef Sudbrack, SJ, "Mystik als Lerngebiet der Meditation," *Geist und Leben* 49 (1976): 383–89.
[24] January 4, 1978.

was the question of death and resurrection. This was the only subject on which he read exegetical literature.[25] The older he became, the less satisfied he was with the images of the old catechism, in which the hereafter looks almost exactly like this life. *When it comes to the afterlife, I'm like Thomas: unless I see it myself, I don't believe it. All the evidence cannot bring me peace.*[26] In addition, he had long been preoccupied with the question of what would happen to the unbaptized, *the God-haters*, and *the pagans* after death, whether these people would really go to hell. *Since it is theoretically possible for anyone to convert at the hour of death,*[27] he had written in 1955. Now, some twenty-five years and many experiences later, he saw things differently. Someone like the Hindu saint Ramana Maharshi, he thought, was *undoubtedly in heaven and also a saint* to whom one could *ask for intercession.*[28] And when Yamada, the mayor of Hiroshima, whom Lassalle had met already earlier during his studies in England in the 1920s, died, he wrote in his diary: *If a man is really good, that cannot be the end. He lives on.*[29]

Another question arose from the words of the Mass canon: "As this water is mixed with the wine, let us also share in the divinity of Christ," he used to pray when he poured a few drops of water into the wine chalice during Mass. *If Christ is God, then we are also God,*[30] he noted, but also *Christ is unique.*[31]

Out of all these questions came his great interest in India's company of "those already liberated in their lifetime" (*jivan-mukta*), the enlightened saints who had already overcome all

---

[25] For example, Jacob Kremer, *Die Osterevangelien. Geschichten um Geschichte* (Österreichisches Katholisches Bibelwerk, 1977); Xavier Leon-Dufour, *Face a la mort: Jesus et Paul* (Seuil, 1979).

[26] February 4, 1957.

[27] January 10, 1955.

[28] December 13, 1971.

[29] January 22, 1975.

[30] December 15, 1975.

[31] September 13, 1975.

delusion. On his way from Europe to Japan, he visited the Hindu saint Anandamayi Ma (1896–1982)—said to be an incarnation of goddess Durga—in India, considered by many to be the most important saint in India since the death of Sri Aurobindo and Ramana Maharshi.[32] Immediately after his arrival in Delhi, Lassalle traveled north to Haridwar to Anandamayi Ma's ashram and went for *darshan*. *Darshan* refers to the direct encounter with God in a very concrete situation, for example, through the presence of a person. Lassalle first asked for advice on how to practice meditation. The eighty-year-old Ma said that what was necessary was *1. posture, 2. concentration on the breath, 3. emptiness. Regarding 2, she said that you have to come to where the breath comes from . . . Ma kept saying that Atman is one.* She came to "*darshan*" in me, she said, through Lassalle's transparency, his *simplicity and naturalness. After the conversation, I was allowed to sit in front of her for a few minutes.* A deep silence enveloped the thirty or forty people present. Lassalle forgot time and space. The few minutes of meditation turned into an hour and a half, and people later told him that they had never meditated for so long here before. The next day, when Hugo Lassalle came for *darshan*, she sent most of the people out. *I thanked her again and said that when I arrived, I didn't know if she was still there. She said, "You were already here. If you weren't already here, you couldn't have come."*[33] In conversation, *she playfully moved from one dimension to another.* In the afternoon, before Lassalle drove back to Delhi, she called him out of the crowd that had gathered and gave him *prasad*, a flower, and fruit.

The next few months were difficult for Father Lassalle. He was supposed to renew his driving license but forgot to do so,

---

[32] cf. Melita Maschmann, *Eine ganz gewöhnliche Heilige* (Otto Wilhelm Barth Verlag, 1992 (expanded new edition of *Der Tiger singt Kirtan,* 1967).
[33] April 21, 1976.

and now, at the age of seventy-eight, he had to retake the driving test. After twenty-three failed attempts, he finally passed the test in March of the following year. As best he could, he took the repeated attempts as a spiritual practice. He would rather fast strictly according to the old rules during Lent, he realized before the last test, than endure this testing situation.

At the end of June 1977, Lassalle held a sesshin in Pakistan with the Dominicans north of Rawalpindi at an altitude of 2,200 meters. In Pakistan, Sufi mysticism still characterizes the religiosity of a large part of the population. Immediately after his arrival in Lahore, Lassalle met a Sufi sheik, a young man who was *very natural* and *unpretentious*.[34] He brought Lassalle to a Sufi saint the next day. He was of *great simplicity, openness, honesty*, and lived in poor circumstances, but was not as thin as the Shankaracharya of Kanchi, but had a pot belly, as Lassalle noted. Both Sufis said that *truth could neither be grasped by concepts nor expressed in words*.[35] It was transmitted through the spiritual bond between master and disciple. *The element of love was particularly strong, in the sense of love for God*.[36] When Lassalle returned to Japan after two weeks in Pakistan, he suffered from memory loss: *Where you don't see clearly, you remember something that wasn't there. And where you don't remember the daily routine*.[37] But the disturbance soon subsided.

Meanwhile, Lassalle was becoming increasingly well known in Europe, and sometimes more foreigners than Japanese attended the sesshins in Shinmeikutsu. Through Lassalle's mediation, many Christians from Europe also sat in Yamada Roshi's Zendo in Kamakura to complete koan training and become Zen teachers: the Pallottine Johannes Kopp, the Benedictine

---

[34] June 30, 1977.
[35] June 30, 1977.
[36] July 1, 1977.
[37] July 24, 1977.

Willigis Jäger, the Jesuit Niklaus Brantschen, the Franciscan Victor Löw, the Protestant pastor Gundula Meyer, the Benedictine Ludwigis Fabian, Pia Gyger from the Katharinawerk, and a whole series of other priests, all a generation younger than Hugo Lassalle. Until then Yamada Roshi had given Lassalle as many dokusan as possible so that he could complete the koans quickly. But now he needed time for the other Western students; moreover, the dokusan with Father Lassalle always took a long time because he needed more detailed explanations than other students because of his teaching activities. Lassalle felt that receiving fewer dokusan was a breach of Roshi's promise to go through the koans with him as quickly as possible.

His wish was to establish Zen practice as an integral part of Christian practice in Europe. In Germany, the first Christian meditation center was opened in 1974 in Tholey, Saarland, by the local Benedictine monastery. In the "Exercitium Humanum" under the direction of Willi Massa (1931–2001), a broad spectrum of activities was pursued, ranging from Zen practice and eutony to depth psychology workshops. But what Lassalle had in mind was a house where the practice of silence and contemplation would dominate the atmosphere. On Christmas Day, December 27, 1977, Lassalle, together with the Bishop of Eichstätt (Upper Bavaria), was able to inaugurate a new meditation house in an old Franciscan monastery in Dietfurt in the Altmühl valley. On the foundations of the old cloistered yard, a large Zendo was built, combining Japanese and European styles, with a large baroque cross from the dining hall of the Franciscan monastery hanging on the front wall.

The goal of Zen is "the experience of God," Lassalle emphasized in his homily at the dedication, and that experience can be personal or impersonal. "We cannot limit God. God is not this or that, he is everything." The crucial thing, he said, is to go to the ground of one's being, to the "bottom of the soul," as the mystics say. "In this ground, we can experience God. And

Fr. Enomiya-Lassalle together with his friend, the Franciscan priest Fr. Victor Löw, who built the first zendo in a Christian monastery in the baroque Franciscan convent of Dietfurt, Germany. This was the first zendo in a Christian context, open for all who wanted to practice.

in this ground alone, all our weaknesses and imperfections are gradually dissolved. . . . They were not thinking of some great experience, no, they were thinking of perfection on the Christian path." Zen practice is about the transformation and maturation of the whole person. Zen meditation, says Lassalle, "if practiced correctly, faithfully and strictly—and under someone who has experience—offers the certainty of reaching this ground," some more slowly, others more quickly. The fact that the Zen House in Dietfurt is located "in a Christian, Catholic monastery" is the best basis for this development. Even though Zen is in the foreground, this does not exclude other types of meditation from being practiced here. "Everyone should find what he needs at the moment." It seems that rational thinking is losing its dominance and that more and more people are looking for the experience of "the ground" and want to live from this experience. "Then we will finally achieve world peace."[38]

---

[38] Unpublished manuscript.

9

"All I Wanted Was to Help People, Nothing Else"

❧

In the fall and winter of 1977, Germany was experiencing serious social conflict. Large demonstrations by environmentalists protesting nuclear power plants in Brokdorf in the north of Germany and Kalkar at the Rhine were met with police violence. The militant left wing "Red Army Faction" assassinated high-ranking representatives of the German late capitalist society, leading to an increased state force presence. Lassalle wrote a letter to a woman horrified by the situation. He replied, "Are these young people really 100 percent evil? One thing is indisputable: they do not fear death. In other words, they are prepared to risk their lives. Who is to blame for these people being the way they are? Does not all of humanity share some of the blame? Let us not forget to pray for these people, too. They are also children of God."[1] Every human being is a child of God and has part in God. Therefore, every human being deserves

---

[1] Letter to Ms. R., Tokyo, November 7, 1977.

to be loved as the image of God, regardless of who they are. Hugo Lassalle treated every human being with this attitude, whether it was a person sentenced to death for murder whom Lassalle accompanied for years until his death, or a Jesuit who had secretly left the order, married, and was now dying—abandoned by all—whom Lassalle took into his care, or one of his students in trouble. He always had an open ear and, if possible and necessary, helped in a concrete way.

This does not mean that he accepted everything uncritically. On the contrary, he had very strict moral standards. The measure of these standards was selflessness in all things, in small, everyday tasks, as well as major matters. In his dealings with others, this meant humility and respect for everyone. He also demanded this of his Zen students to the best of their ability. However, when it came to Zen practice, Lassalle's perspective went far beyond this. He hoped for a fundamental transformation of human consciousness, beginning with the individual and gradually leading to widespread change.

Considering the significant progress in physical, chemical, biological, and medical research since the beginning of the twentieth century—ranging from the utilization of atomic energy to the development of plastics, information technologies, and genetic engineering—this assumption was not unexpected. Unprecedented opportunities for shaping one's own life and the world were becoming available. "For the first time ever, a living being understands its origins and can shape its own future," wrote an American molecular biologist in the late 1960s.[2] What was missing were the criteria for doing so. The image that humanity had of itself was undergoing a profound change. Karl Marx and Friedrich Nietzsche had already

---

[2] Daniel J. Kevles, "Die Geschichte der Genetik und Eugenik," in *Der Supercode: Die genetische Karte des Menschen*, ed. Daniel J. Kevles and Leroy Hood (Insel Taschenbuch, 1995), 29.

diagnosed this phenomenon from different perspectives in the nineteenth century. For Lassalle, his encounter with the Swiss cultural philosopher Jean Gebser was a decisive factor. According to Gebser, Asian cultures are neither exotic nor intellectually inferior to Europe; they are not a threat to European identity either. The encounter between Asia and Europe is part of a comprehensive shift in consciousness, according to Gebser.

Such shifts in collective consciousness have occurred frequently in the past. For instance, the realization that an image of an object or symbol can be used instead of the object itself, for example, in the case of a burial object, marks such a shift. The discovery of the centralized perspective at the beginning of the modern era is another indication of a shift in consciousness.

For Gebser, the replacement of the centralized perspective by an aperspectival view in modern art, as well as advances in contemporary physics, are indications of an emerging shift in consciousness in our times from rational consciousness to arational or aperspectival consciousness.[3] Lassalle first heard these ideas in 1967 at the conference at Elmau Castle. Such reflections on the impending "mutation of humanity"[4] were a topic that preoccupied many intellectuals at the time.

Physicist and Nobel Prize winner Heisenberg confirmed Lassalle's belief that integrating the fourth dimension of time would lead to a transformation in consciousness. Lassalle believed that this new consciousness would be supported by *the experience of the absolute*.[5] Those who live from this experience simply emanate it, even in a concentration camp.

After visiting the Dachau Nazi concentration camp, he

---

[3] Jean Gebser, *Ursprung und Gegenwart*, 3 vols. (Deutsche Verlags-Anstalt, 1949).

[4] For example, the very successful musical *Hair* addresses these expectations.

[5] March 9, 1974.

wrote, *The individual will radiate it, even if he is sitting in a concentration camp like Dachau. He lives beyond life and death. His tormentors could not escape his influence. It doesn't matter what background someone comes from, whether it be Christianity, Buddhism, yoga, TM, or anything else. All of these should feel united as stones of the Kingdom of God.* This fundamental transformation of consciousness is the basis for peace on earth. *The "against" must disappear: against yoga . . . against Christianity . . . against communism . . . Only "for" should remain. In this, everyone should be free.*[6]

The Gospel of Thomas, which literally emerged from the desert sands in 1945 alongside an entire ancient library, supported Lassalle's ideas. The Jesus of the Gospel of Thomas often speaks in paradoxes that could have come from an ancient Zen master. This lost gospel, whose authenticity is still disputed by researchers today,[7] became an important guide for Lassalle in his belief that certain changes were necessary for humanity to prosper. Lassalle was certain that this shift in consciousness would affect the Catholic Church as well. After all, traditional images of God were providing people with less and less guidance. *The many gods had to die [. . .] and finally, so did the one God. In their place came concepts that are nothing in themselves. Suddenly, people are finding that these concepts are unsatisfying and that conceptual thought alone does not bring peace. They are searching for the true reality behind the concepts.*[8] The *true reality behind the concepts* cannot be expressed in traditional theological language. Therefore, one must return to the sources: the Gospels and the person of Jesus, who reveals himself through them. The only way to do so is "through one's

---

[6] October 4, 1975.

[7] The Gospel of Thomas, a collection of sayings by Jesus, is among the texts discovered in Nag Hammadi, Egypt in 1945. A noncanonical text, it is thought to be influenced by Gnosticism.

[8] September 9, 1982.

own religious experience, found in deep prayer and contemplation. There, Christ himself can give us answers directly."[9] This path is not bound to any institution. "I am increasingly convinced that it is not God who imposes boundaries, but man himself. God is always ready to give everyone what can be given to a human being,"[10] Lassalle wrote in a letter. His personal vision was a new religious order combining contemplation and practical work for the poor—an order without statutes, similar to the initial concept of Ignatius of Loyola.[11]

Lassalle summarized these thoughts in a book about the emergence of the new consciousness (1981, English translation: *Living in a New Consciousness,* 1988). A Japanese fellow Jesuit brother complained about the book in Rome, forcing Lassalle to take a stand on "objective values" and the "magisterium of the Church." "Your work is held in the highest esteem and was explicitly supported at the second meeting of the FABC[12] in November 1978," read the reply from Rome.[13] That settled the matter, though Lassalle is still criticized for it by some church circles today.[14]

Lassalle endured these and other problems with church institutions as best he could. For him, something else was far more important: his immediate relationship with Jesus Christ and his inner sense of connection with him. Only in the last years of his life did he write about this in more detail in his diaries. This personal relationship with Christ, however, accompanied and guided Lassalle throughout his entire life. It was fundamental to him.

---

[9] Hugo M. Enomiya-Lassalle, *Am Morgen einer besseren Welt: Der Mensch im Durchbruch zu einem neuen Bewusstsein* (Herderbucherei, 1984), 154.

[10] Letter to Rev. Martin, Karachi, Tokyo, October 30, 1977.

[11] May 7, 1978.

[12] Federation of Asian Bishops Conference.

[13] Letter from Paolo Dezza, March 22, 1982.

[14] The German Jesuit Josef Sudbrack, who criticized Lassalle's work from the outset, expressly rejects the book as suspected New Age.

Toward the end of his life, he discovered the feminine and the possibility of entering into relationships with women. *This was only a few years ago, so relatively late, perhaps a consequence of the upbringing I had in my youth,*[15] he wrote in his diary. However, the intimate relationship with Christ remained foundational. This was partly due to the fact that, over the years, he had developed a new way of reading the Bible. He saw what was behind the words. He called this "seeing through": *I experienced it almost as if it had taken place before my eyes. It was not a vision, but something like it. Therefore, there can be no doubt about it.*[16] This quality of perception was also shared by those who participated in the Eucharist, which he celebrated daily during the sesshins.

This became particularly evident during Holy Week. The Holy Week sesshin always took place at the St. Franziskus meditation center in Dietfurt. Unlike usual, the liturgy was part of the sesshin. Everyone sat on the floor in the chapel, including Lassalle. In front of him stood a small table with a missal and chalice, a candle and flowers in front of it, and behind it on the wall a cross and the tabernacle. There was only the text of the missal, no singing and no sermon. The deep silence of the sesshin continued in the liturgy. The story of the Passion, the story of devotion and betrayal, of torture, pain, suffering, and hopelessness, and of liberation and resurrection, became real in an unfathomable way. When Father Lassalle threw himself to the ground and stretched out his long, tired body during the veneration of the cross on Good Friday, there was nothing but a broken man, but at the same time, a presence whose profound vitality and love overcame all despair and death. On Holy Saturday, when the liturgy of the Resurrection had ended, and everyone in the chapel stood in silence around the burning

---

[15] January 6, 1980.
[16] March 1, 1980.

Easter candle, he came and said, "Happy Easter," and then left the chapel smiling.

In his diary, he once wrote. *The resurrected Christ can still walk through closed doors today—whether it is Zen or even atheism.*[17]

Lassalle was aware that death was approaching. His sister Maria, with whom he was very close, died in April 1978 after a long illness. On the day of her death, her brother was filled with a great sense of unease, which he took as a sign of her passing. His other sister, Lisbeth, died seven years later.

The news of his old friend Peter Winter's death came as a shock to the eighty-year-old. For Lassalle's birthday, the Mainz religious educator Gunter Stachel published an anthology: *Munen Muso: Ungegenständliche Meditation* [Formless Meditation], a collection of essays on the topic that is now out of print but highly recommended. Yamada Roshi contributed an essay in which he *"challenged"* Christians, especially those who had attained kensho, *to clarify how they could incorporate the Buddhist concept of emptiness.*[18] Lassalle had always believed that the experience of enlightenment was similar for Christians and Buddhists, despite their different linguistic and mental contexts. For example, the Spanish Jesuit Carlos M. Staehlin had called this experience "transcendental consciousness," or the intrusion of the "supraconsciousness," in an article in the early 1960s in the Jesuit magazine *Geist und Leben* (*Spirit and Life*). In this experience, he wrote, one abandons all words, images, and mental concepts and surrenders to nothingness.[19] This roughly corresponds to the interpretation of enlightenment found in the philosopher and Zen expert D. T. Suzuki, who describes it as an "immediate experience" not

---

[17] March 30, 1982.

[18] January 30, 1978.

[19] Carlos Maria Staehlin, SJ, "Mystische Täuschungen, Zur Beurteilung einiger mystischer Phänomene," *Geist und Leben* (1954): 276–90, 277.

bound to any specific religion or culture. This view is also held by Kitaro Nishida and other philosophers of the Kyoto School, and has been popularized in the West by D. T. Suzuki.

For Lassalle, it was conceivable that someone could have an experience of God through the koan "Mu" and thereby resolve it. He repeatedly asked Yamada Roshi how to assess Europeans who were unfamiliar with Buddhist terms such as "Buddha nature" or "Mu" yet had experienced God in Zen practice. The roshi replied that he should let these people *practice Mu; then, they would gradually find clarity.*[20]

"Mu," just like "Buddha nature," is a valid equivalent to the central Buddhist term *sunyata*, or emptiness. Thus, it has a long history in Buddhist thought, just as "God" and "experience of God" are terms with a long history. Lassalle appreciated the attempt of some of Yamada Koun Roshi's Christian students to equate "Buddha nature" with the concept of the "cosmic Christ" because it *aligned closely with the Buddhist perspective on the unity of the world of appearances and absolute reality.*[21] For him, it was clear: *In meditation, the idea came to me right at the beginning: Christ is in me.*[22] Apart from that, he was looking for a completely new way of expression appropriate to the transformation of consciousness at that time, one that went back to the anthropological basis of the worlds of Christianity and Buddhism. This undertaking met with much criticism from Christian and Buddhist authorities. Conversely, it was precisely for this reason that he was invited to conferences promoting dialogue between science and religion.

In 1979, Yamada Roshi commissioned Lassalle to write an introduction to Zen practice for Europeans. During their conversations, the roshi discussed the conditions under which

---

[20] October 24, 1980.
[21] September 15, 1979.
[22] September 14, 1979.

other European Christians could obtain a teaching permission as Zen teachers. The roshi said that *gojukai*, the ordination for lay people to the five *sila*, that is, the fundamental Buddhist precepts, should be omitted because it makes one a disciple of Buddha. His view of Japanese Zen was somewhat pessimistic. Japanese Zen Buddhism seemed institutionally weak to him and was losing touch with the experience of enlightenment. He viewed Christian churches, particularly the Catholic Church, as ideal vessels for preserving and disseminating the Zen tradition—"a transmission outside of scripture, directly from heart to heart," as it is referred to.[23] Most of the "Westerners" whom Yamada Koun Roshi later, in the 1980s, granted permission to teach Zen were Christian theologians and ministers from Catholic and Protestant churches. By doing so, Yamada Roshi took a unique historical step: he formally conferred the official powers of the Zen Buddhist tradition on officials of the Protestant and Catholic branches of Christianity. However, they were not to bear the title "roshi," as this title authorizes one to perform Buddhist ceremonies, as he pointed out to Father Lassalle.[24] Since "a cup of tea tastes the same to Buddhists and Christians," as Yamada Roshi paraphrased the experience of kensho or enlightenment, Christians should also be allowed to teach Zen as a path to enlightenment.

Lassalle completed the koan practice according to the Sanbokyodan school's criteria in 1979 and was the first Christian to get teaching permission. Before his next trip to Europe, the roshi gave Lassalle precise instructions on how to perform *shoken*, the small ceremony with which a Zen master accepts a new student. However, Lassalle never officially accepted any-

---

[23] Communication from Migaku Sato; *cf.* Yamada Koun, "Über das Christentum, über die Welt und über die Zukunft," in *Übung der Kontemplation: Christen gehen den Zen-Weg*, ed. Günter Stachel (Matthias-Grünewald-Verl, 1988), 166–72.

[24] August 14, 1983.

one as a student during all those years. During his lectures at sesshins, he explained that he was in Europe too infrequently to do so. Yet, a glance at the list of sesshins reveals that, between 1979 and 1990, Lassalle spent more time in Europe than in Japan. Although Lassalle wanted official recognition as a Zen teacher—confirmation that he was part of the Zen tradition—the decision not to take on the role of "master," or roshi, may have been made early on. According to Buddhist belief, the roshi embodies the "absolute"; he is a living Buddha. While there have always been spiritual teachers in Christianity, they have never described themselves as the embodiment of God or Christ. Already soon after his first sesshin with Yamada Roshi, Lassalle wrote in his diary: *In today's Gospel, Matthew 23:1-12, "You shall not be called Rabbi," I thought involuntarily: You shall not be called Roshi, for one is a Roshi: Christ.*[25]

Yamada Roshi encouraged Lassalle to conduct kensho assessments in Europe. However, he reserved the right to grant approval himself. During the assessments, Lassalle forgot to ask some of the specified questions and could not recall all of the answers. Therefore, the roshi demanded that Lassalle repeat all of the koans but allowed him to continue working with his course participants using koans. The roshi wanted to continue assessing kenshos himself. However, Yamada Roshi found less and less time to give Lassalle the necessary dokusan for the repetition. Since 1981, many Europeans had completed their koan practice in his zendo and received teaching permission, while others were nearing the end of their training. Lassalle also spent many months of the year in Europe.

Perhaps the reason Roshi Yamada requires only me to repeat all the koans is because he believes that I am influenced by scholastic philosophy in a way that no one else is. After all, they are from a later generation and have neither stud-

---

[25] February 20, 1973.

ied philosophy nor theology.[26] Repeating the koans was stressful for Lassalle because some Europeans in Yamada Roshi's zendo mocked him behind his back for doing so. This sometimes drove him to despair, but he did not become embittered. Following Christ and practicing the "third degree of humility" remained his way of life. Living by his motto, *ama nesciri et pro nihilo putari*, was not easy for him. Loving being unknown and being considered nothing was the most radical practice of non-self in everyday life.

Perhaps it was precisely this humble acceptance of his own weakness that encouraged the many people who came into contact with Lassalle. They saw in him the courage to live and the courage to embark on a spiritual path. His card index showed that around four thousand people regularly attended his sesshins. According to statistics that Lassalle compiled for his order's Superior General Arrupe in 1980, he held thirty-four sesshins in Europe in this year. A total of 1,223 people attended these sesshin, 56 percent of whom were women and 44 percent of whom were men. The attendees came from all walks of life, though there was a slight prevalence of the educated middle class. More than half of the participants were between thirty and fifty years old. Lassalle noted that the younger participants, in particular, had lost contact with the church.

In Spain, during the fall of 1981, between sesshins, Lassalle visited the places where the two great mystics, Teresa of Ávila and John of the Cross, had worked. Ana María Schlüter Rodés, who started building a Zen group in Spain in 1978 and regularly practiced koan with Yamada Roshi in Kamakura, organized these sesshins. There was an opportunity to attend a bullfight in between sesshins—Lassalle was fascinated but also repulsed.

Lassalle had been suffering from severe dizziness and stomach pains while traveling for some time, but the doctor he con-

---

[26] May 9, 1982.

sulted could not find anything wrong. After the New Year's sesshin in Shinmeikutsu in 1983, Lassalle flew to Europe with a fever. He was so weak that the flight attendants took his hand luggage. Upon arriving in Dietfurt, he was diagnosed with severe pneumonia and was confined to bed for a long time. He was unable to lead another sesshin until Easter.

The doctors in Germany confirmed that Lassalle had made a full recovery. Back in Tokyo, his superiors ordered him to undergo a medical examination, which also confirmed his good health.

During those years, someone must have given him a pair of woolen socks. Lassalle took them and put them in his closet. He wanted to save them for old age, said the man, who was now over eighty. Later, near the end of his life, he actually used them. He was still traveling from one sesshin to another, from one continent to another. Sometimes, on these lonely journeys, he lost heart. But he thought, *One just has to start, and it will work out.*[27] That was also the advice he gave to those who came to him in despair. "That can happen. Just keep going." This advice helped, and perhaps it helped because it was said with a sense of security that he had had to fight for again and again. *The Imitation of Christ* helped him, as did the saying he found in the mystic John of the Cross and the Zen master Dogen: *Nothing to hope for. Nothing to fear. Nothing to rejoice in. Nothing to be sad about.*[28]

Wherever he could, he supported members of religious orders so they could practice Zen in Kamakura or build their own zendo. For example, he supported Johannes Kopp (1927–2016) in Germany, A. M. Arokiasamy (1936–) in India, Ana Maria Schlüter Rodés (1935–) in Spain, and Sister Elaine McInnes in the Philippines. He mediated between the then-

---

[27] February 16, 1984.
[28] January 28, 1984.

young Japanese theologian, Migaku Sato (1948–)[29] and his university teacher, who was also a Japanese Christian and refused to accept that Sato practiced Zen. He helped where he could. "He was often the angel in disguise that some people needed," writes a former student.[30] Sometimes, that simply meant reading to someone who was ill or bringing someone food.

Yet these years were anything but easy for Lassalle. The situation in Kamakura did not improve for him, even though the roshi said, "Although Father Lassalle is my Zen student, I can say from the bottom of my heart that he is my master in life. His deep humility, generosity, and humanity are qualities that I deeply admire and appreciate."[31]

In addition, he was undergoing a long-lasting process of transformation. The old image of a concrete God disappeared more and more. He found himself in a liminal state. *The gap between the disappearance of the concrete God and a new, positive* [. . .] was sometimes *suddenly filled,* [. . .] *an inner oneness existed,*[32] but then this experience faded, and Lassalle continued walking through inner darkness. *One night, the words came to me of their own accord: God, my God, why have you forsaken me? I thought: Perhaps there is a God after all, as I used to believe? I would not regret it.*[33]

The fear that had plagued him all his life still refused to go away. *I have to live with "fear." People who know me don't notice it, but they don't really know me deep down. I am a cripple, but my friends and admirers don't see or believe it. I am still a child, undeveloped, and not in a positive sense. On*

---

[29] Migaku Sato is professor emeritus for New Testament at Rikkyo University, Tokyo, and roshi of Sanbo-Zen-School.

[30] Reported from Peter Zehnder.

[31] Niklaus Brantschen, "Ein Mann mit einem großen Herzen," in *In Memoriam Koun Yamada* (Sambo Koryukai, Kamakura 1997), 11.

[32] February 15, 1986.

[33] March 28, 1986.

the other hand, I am richly gifted spiritually. But that is my
secret, and it will probably remain so until I die.[34]

His schedule was as busy as ever. He sometimes suffered
from shortness of breath and feared suffocation. His stomach
was also becoming increasingly sensitive. However, these
issues did not prevent him from *continuing. I have the feeling*
that I am open on all sides, i.e., that there are no boundaries.
[. . .] With respect to "open to all sides," I don't know if that
[. . .] is a further step in integrating the new consciousness.
Perhaps it will become clearer. Instead of "open to all sides,"
one could also say "no either or." However, that doesn't mean
one feels comfortable in every situation.[35]

In mid-January 1985, Lassalle flew to India, but he had
forgotten to get a visa. So, he flew on to Kathmandu. While
waiting in line at the Indian embassy, a young Nepalese man
suddenly tried to snatch the elderly foreigner's shoulder bag.
Lassalle did not let go of the bag, and the young man dragged
him a few meters until he gave up. With the help of the taxi
driver who had taken him to the embassy and looked after
him attentively, Lassalle was finally able to obtain a visa.
The eighty-seven-year-old also encountered helpful people in
India, where he traveled on crowded buses and trains as usual.
He visited Bede Griffiths in Shantivanam once more and held
some sesshins for Jesuit novices and nuns in Dindigul and
Madras. Then, he flew from Mumbai via Athens to Tel Aviv.
There, he traveled through the "Holy Land" with Father Victor
Löw and the Indian Jesuit A. M. Arokyasamy, who had just
received his authorization as Zen teacher. Between sesshins in
the Netherlands, Germany, and Spain, Lassalle visited Pastor
Gundula Meyer (1937–), who had also just begun teaching.
In the morning, Lassalle celebrated Mass as usual and asked

---

[34] February 1, 1987.
[35] May 5, 1987.

Gundula—a woman and a Protestant—if she would like to join him in celebrating the Eucharist according to an ecumenical text. She only wanted to assist because she was not familiar with the text. Between the sesshin, he also visited his friend P. Johannes Kopp in Essen, who had also received teaching permission. He traveled from one sesshin to the next, visiting Dietfurt, Paris, Rome, Tokyo, Kyoto, Shinmeikutsu, Amsterdam, and Madrid. His health was not the best. During a sesshin in Erfurt, still under communist rule in the German Democratic Republic, he had a nosebleed that lasted from night until morning. He also suffered from occasional shortness of breath, but that did not stop him.

At the end of October 1988, Lassalle inaugurated in Spain Ana Maria Schlüter Rodés's new Zen center in Brihuega near Madrid. At that time, it was still a temporary facility—a decommissioned greenhouse. He also celebrated his ninetieth birthday there. For a few moments, he was alone in Ana Maria Schlüter's small house. Music played on the radio, and he began to dance by himself. The music moved him deeply. But when someone approached the house, he stopped immediately.

"The fact that all these Catholic people are practicing zazen today is only possible because Father Lassalle broke the ice," wrote Yamada Roshi. The goal of Buddhism, he says, "is to liberate all living beings. But that is impossible for Buddhism today. We must work together with the Catholic Church. Without cooperation, we cannot achieve this goal."[36] Liberation from dualistic thinking leads to peace and unity in the world. Only in this way can poverty be eliminated worldwide, the roshi wrote. Even though Yamada Roshi and Hugo Lassalle had a difficult relationship when it came to koan practice, they

---

[36] Yamada Kōun Roshi, Über das Christentum, über die Welt und über die Zukunft," in *Übung der Kontemplation: Christen gehen den Zen-Weg*, ed. Günter Stachel (Matthias-Grünewald-Verl, 1988), 168ff.

agreed that Zen should contribute to a new, peaceful world.

Lassalle had previously thought it would be nice to *pass away into eternity* after his ninetieth birthday. In the spring of 1989, he underwent surgery for colon cancer. While still recovering, he moved to Dietfurt in May but was unable to hold sesshin.

"Nothing to hope for, nothing to fear" is probably the best attitude for getting through the current crisis. Things may well remain this way until the end of my life. I don't blame anyone. After all, the situation is not unbearable, and I don't feel abandoned, even when I pray. I can't expect anything from the people in Dietfurt regarding this matter. I could not talk to anyone here about it. On the other hand, I am grateful that I [can] be here without having to work. That will [. . .] surely come to an end.[37]

Yamada Roshi passed away on September 13, 1989. After falling in the autumn of 1988, he was seriously injured and paralyzed. Lassalle wanted to lead one more sesshin, but he contracted an infection and developed a high fever. On September 27, he held his final dokusan. Lassalle was weak but willing *to carry on*, even though he knew he *had to be prepared for anything*. He was on his way into the "dark night" of godforsakenness.

However, when in the spring of 1989 the opposition against the communist regime in Eastern Germany grew stronger and in November the Berlin Wall fell, he said enthusiastically that it was worth growing so old after all.

At Christmas, he received a document from the new Sanbokyodan board with a Zen name for him: Ai-un, Cloud of Love. In mid-March 1990, Lassalle fell and broke his femur, requiring another operation. In mid-May, he had to move from Dietfurt to the Jesuit retirement home in Münster.

---

[37] June 27, 1989.

The notes in his diary from this period are fragmentary, often just scraps of thoughts that give a glimpse of the distress of his situation. *A retirement home is a difficult place. I have not yet figured out if there is another solution or another way . . . to move forward.*[38] This is followed by a very long dash. It is the final entry in the diary. In the following six weeks, many came to say goodbye. "Where there is dead meat, the vultures come," Lassalle commented on the situation.

At the end of June, he underwent another operation for an intestinal obstruction. His old assistant and friend, Masanori Some, came to care for him, taking turns with other friends. Hugo Lassalle regained consciousness one last time. He was in great pain and could hardly speak.

Fr. Enomiya-Lassalle practicing Zen in the zendo of Shinmeikutsu, in the background his assistant Masanori Some, a former Rinzai monk, who became Catholic.

A week before his death, a visitor came to the hospital to say goodbye to Father Lassalle. He signaled for her to go to the wall cabinet where the Bible lay. She was to read aloud

---

[38] May 18, 1990.

a passage from the New Testament; soon she realized that it should be from Jesus's farewell discourse to his disciples in the Gospel of John, "Because he loved them, he loved them to the end." Before the Last Supper, Jesus, the Lord and Master, washed his disciples' feet. "I have given you an example that you should do as I have done to you" (John 13:1, 15).

On Saturday afternoon, July 7, 1990, Hugo Lassalle passed away. "Great God, we praise you. Lord, we praise your strength. Before you, the earth bows down and admires your works. As You were before all time, so You will remain forever." Everyone in the room sang the Te Deum. It was Hugo Lassalle's favorite song. He stopped breathing at the end of the first verse.

According to Japanese custom, Hugo Lassalle's body was cremated, and the urn was transferred to the Peace Memorial Church in Hiroshima. The Requiem Mass took place on July 12 in Münster.

Conclusion

The seeds planted by Father Lassalle′s exemplary life have sprouted and are still growing. More than half a century later, Zen practice among Christians is still flourishing and blossoming, even though it is not for everyone. Contemplation has never been a mass movement, just as in Buddhist countries Zen practice, Vipassana, and other paths are not followed by everyone.

When Father Lassalle attended a Zen sesshin in 1943, he was in search for a way of prayer suitable for Japanese Catholics, who disliked verbose Western prayer. Due to the political situation, he was permitted to participate in an otherwise prohibited non-Catholic religious activity, provided he had no personal religious motivation.

He was certainly not aware that he was beginning to break a ban that had crippled Christian spirituality for more than 300 years. During the Golden Age of Spanish mysticism, in the sixteenth century, Teresa of Ávila and John of the Cross taught contemplation to their convents and lay people. Around the middle of the seventeenth century, a fierce theological— or even ideological—debate about the value of contemplation resulted in the Quietist controversy, which finally culminated in the condemnation of "Quietism" as a heresy in 1687 by Pope Innocent XI in the papal encyclical *Coelistis pastor*, and by the inquisition under Pope Innocent XII in 1699. Contemplation, or quiet prayer without verbal content, went underground.[1] The ban on wordless prayer was effective, and spiritual practice and piety focused more and more on images, words, and rituals, such as the rosary, devotion to the Sacred Heart of Jesus, and other forms of pious activity.

Although Lassalle studied the Spanish mystics in his tertianship before his final vows as a Jesuit, he did not learn how to practice contemplation. Instead, he learned "reflective prayer," as recommended in neo-scholastic spirituality.[2] For him, this was not deep enough in times of crisis and stress. It was not until the early 1950s that he began practicing inner silence as he had learned during the 1943 sesshin. When he began practicing in Buddhist temples, he discovered a wealth of sources in the premodern spiritual tradition of Christian mysticism that offered a way of spirituality beyond words and images. His main references were, besides John of the Cross, Johannes Tauler, Jan van Ruusbroec, Richard Rolle, and the Cloud of Unknowing.[3] The latter was translated into English by his fellow Jesuit, William Johnston, a project which Lassalle encouraged.

When his first account of Zen practice as a Christian, *Zen: Way to Enlightenment*, was published in 1961 and translated into English, Spanish, French, Dutch, Japanese, and Korean, it met an audience with an obvious but unspoken need for silence and contemplation. The Second Vatican Council, with its documents *Nostra Aetate* (§ 2) and *Ad Gentes* (§ 18), paved the way for this new endeavor, which transcended traditional church piety. When I met him as a young student in 1976, full of doubts about my Catholic upbringing, I gained a new understanding simply through the pain in my legs and back during

---

[1] Karl Baier, *Meditation und Moderne*, vol. 1 (Königshausen & Neuman, 2009), 157–78.
[2] Baier., vol. 2, 543–58.
[3] See also Hugo M. Enomiya-Lassalle, *Zen-Buddhismus,* 3rd ed. (Bachem, 1974).

hours of Zen practice. I understood that Zen practice is a way for Christians to participate in death and resurrection, as Paul says in Romans 6:3–6: an understanding beyond any theory or theology, simply through this very body–mind experience. I went on to study philosophy, read Buddhist and Christian texts, and practiced Zen with Lassalle. After his death, I continued practicing with other teachers. Now that I am allowed to guide others in their Zen practice, I strive to uphold his legacy.

Of course, there were many others like me: young and older people searching for a spiritual path. Through Lassalle and others, but mainly by way of the encounter with Zen, from the 1970s onward Christian mysticism was rediscovered. Paperback series of foundational texts were published, and people began practicing meditation. New Christian practices, such as "Centering Prayer," and old Christian practices, such as "Prayer of the Heart," became familiar spiritual paths. It was a sea change, in fact: not the mortification of the body and senses as in traditional asceticism, but the transformation of the senses through selflessness. The years of Vatican II (1962–1965) and the years between then and John Paul II's election as pope in 1978, as well as 1978/1979, the year of the Islamic Revolution in Iran, were a period of great spiritual openness and growth. These were the years where Zen could take roots as a practice among Christians. *Zen unter Christen* (*Zen Meditation for Christians*) is also the title of a widely translated book by Father Lassalle.

Starting in the 1980s, many of the first generation of Christians authorized to teach Zen in Europe, India, the Philippines, and the Americas established Zen centers and laid the institutional groundwork for future growth. In Germany and Switzerland, it was Father Lassalle and several others: Lutheran pastor Gundula Meyer (1937–); Benedictine monk Willigis Jäger (1925–2020, exclaustrated in 2002); Benedictine Ludwigis Fabian (1933–2016); Pallotine Johannes Kopp

(1927–2016); the Catholic theologian and priest Peter Lengsfeld (1930–2009), the Franciscan Victor Löw (d. 1994), who founded the first Christian Zen-Center, the Meditationshaus St. Franziskus (1977) in Germany with support of Father Lassalle; Jesuit Niklaus Brantschen (1937–) in Switzerland; and others. In Spain, Ana Maria Schlüter Rodés (1935–) from the Ladies of Bethany founded Zendo Betania in Brihuega, Spain in 1986, with the support of Father Lassalle. And in India, the Jesuit Arul Maria Arokiasamy (aka Ama Samy) Samy (1936–) founded the Zendo of Bodhi Sangha in Chennai, Tamil Nadu with his support. In the Philippines, Sister Elaine McInnes and subsequent teachers Nenates Pineda and Rosario Battung (Sister of Paul of Chartres, 1943–2021) started a zendo in Manila with the support of Yamada Koun Roshi, who held sesshins there. In the US, Rubén Habito (1947–) and Maria Reis Habito founded the Maria Kannon zendo in Houston, Texas. In Latin America, Ana Maria Schlüter Rodés went to Mexico in 1990, and later her group spread from there to Nicaragua, El Salvador, Guatemala, Ecuador, and Argentina, where Father Lassalle has also become known through the Spanish translation of his books.

All of these people were authorized by Yamada Koun Roshi, Father Lassalle's teacher. However, there were also Christians who became Zen teachers in other lineages. In the Diamond Sangha, for example, the German Lutheran pastor Rolf Drosten was authorized by Robert Aitken Roshi (1917–2010). Aitken had been authorized to teach in 1974 by Yamada Koun Roshi, who made him a Zen Master in 1985. Aitken also authorized the Redemptorist Patrick Hawk (1942–2012). Bernie Glassman Roshi (1939–2018), head of the White Plum Sangha, made the Jesuit Robert E. Kennedy (1933–) a roshi in 1997, as well as Janet Richardson, a Sister of St. Joseph of Peace (1925–) in the same year.

Over the years, these teachers authorized some of their students as Zen teachers. Some of these students were clergy, but most were lay people. Thus, lineages of Zen teachers with Christian backgrounds emerged in Christian, Buddhist, and secular Zen contexts. As Buddhist practices had become more psychologically oriented and therapeutic over the last few decades, this did not bother anyone too much. However, from the time of Pope John Paul II, openness to other religions decreased, resulting in almost no theological reflection on Zen in a Christian context. In addition, the specter of Quietism is still in the air. Interpretations within circles of Christians who practice and teach Zen vary. Some view Zen practice as an addition to Christian spirituality, while others see Zen as a trans-religious practice. More consistent than these inclusive views are those who practice Zen as a Buddhist practice in a Christian context, based on the premise that, like languages, religions refer to the inexpressible mystery, the ultimate reality. Thus, differences should be preserved as they illuminate each other, rather than being mutually exclusive.

When I read Father Lassalle's diaries, which span many thousands of small pages, as I was commissioned by the Japanese Province of the Jesuits to write his biography, I found that Lassalle only held strong opinions in the initial stages of his Zen way. The closer he got to the "center of the labyrinth," the more he held back his opinions and relied on experience. He realized that Christianity and its churches would need to undergo profound changes in their theoretical views in these times of profound mental shifts. These changes would have to come from the heart of Christianity. He writes, "If there is any guarantee at all, it can only be our own religious experience, which we find in deep prayer and contemplation. Only there can the answer be given to us directly by Christ himself."[4]

---

[4] Hugo M. Enomiya-Lassalle, *Am Morgen einer besseren Welt: Der Mensch im Durchbruch zu einem neuen Bewusstsein* (Herderbucherei, 1988), 154.

Afterword

Zen, Christians, and Father Lassalle

The Second Vatican Council's *Nostra Aetate*, also referred to as the *Declaration of the Church on Non-Christian Religions*, makes it known that "the Catholic Church rejects nothing that is true and holy in these religions" and thereby exhorts faithful Christians to "recognize and promote the good things, spiritual and moral, as well as the socio-cultural values found among these" (#2). This Declaration was promulgated at the concluding session of the Second Vatican Council (1965), though it has taken many years after that for this principle and attitude of openness to learning from other religions to be fully accepted at the grassroots level of Christian community life and to be incorporated into Christian self-understanding and practice.

As we learn from this account by Ursula Baatz of Father Hugo Enomiya-Lassalle's life and spiritual journey, he had to muster through many hurdles and obstacles coming from the exclusivistic and triumphalistic attitudes that characterized many in the church at the time, especially clerics and officials, but also many lay people within the Catholic community. In due time though, his persistence, coupled with his humility and totally dedicated way of living his Christian faith, prevailed over these challenges. And now, thanks in great part to his pioneering efforts, many Christians throughout the world drawn to engage in forms of Buddhist practice, seeking to deepen their own spiritual lives, find support and confidence in being able to do so without compromising, and more importantly, while maintaining the integrity of and deepening their own Christian faith and understanding.

It was a blessing and privilege to have been a participant at the Zen retreat (*sesshin*) in Kamakura, Japan in 1974 wherein Father Lassalle was confirmed in his *kensho* experience by Yamada Koun Roshi. It had taken him more than thirty years since he had formally joined a Zen sesshin under a Buddhist master, to finally arrive at this breakthrough with his first koan. During this informal gathering held at the completion of the retreat, as the participants gathered for tea and cookies and conversation, Yamada Roshi, having announced his confirmation of Father Lassalle's Zen experience, offered some pertinent remarks. Speaking to the entire group of us sitting around the Zen hall sipping our tea and munching rice cookies, he acknowledged that Father Lassalle, in his decades of assiduously practicing Zen against a background of Ignatian meditative and contemplative practice that he had been trained in as a Jesuit, had in fact experienced what is referred to in Zen tradition as *kensho*, but with the Western philosophical and theological categories in which he had been intellectually formed, had been unable to connect those experiences within the Zen Buddhist framework whereby *kensho* is checked and identified. Yamada Roshi was now confirming that Father Lassalle did have a genuine Zen *kensho* experience, and had satisfactorily "passed the test" that determined such.

Yamada's own teacher, Yasutani Hakuun Roshi, was known to have declared that in order to practice authentic Zen, those from different (non-Buddhist) backgrounds must leave their (Jewish, Christian, or other) religion at the door as they enter the Zen meditation hall and take on Buddhism as the framework of their spiritual practice. There was a category of meditative practice called "Gedo Zen," literally "outside of the

Way Zen," or "heretical Zen," as it was referred to at the time, the kind that those outside of the Buddhist tradition had been attempting or presuming to practice. This category was among the various kinds of meditative practice listed in the orientation talks offered at the San-un Zendo sangha and marked out as inferior to the authentic Zen that was being offered here.

Yamada Koun Roshi's stance in welcoming Christians to practice Zen under his guidance without asking them to "leave their Christianity at the door" as his own predecessor would have required them to do, coupled with his willingness to listen and learn from them and appreciate what they had to bring into their practice from their own Christian faith tradition, led him to be open to the possibility that Christians might arrive at an authentic Zen experience within their own Christian contexts and thought-frameworks.

Inspired by his open-mindedness and welcoming heart, those who had come to practice Zen under his guidance coming from non-Buddhist backgrounds increased in number through the years. In this particular *sesshin* wherein Father Lassalle's Zen experience was confirmed, out of forty or so total number of participants, there must have been twelve to fifteen at least who were Christian, including ordained Catholic priests or Protestant pastors, women religious, and some lay Christians, with a few Jewish participants in the group as well. At Zen retreats at the San-un Zendo in Kamakura, it had become the custom during chanting time in the morning for the Christian participants to be allowed to celebrate the Eucharist at another room separate from the Zendo with an ordained priest presiding, while the rest of the participants stayed in the Zendo chanting the usual Buddhist sutras. In many of these instances of morning Eucharist during *sesshin*, it was Father Lassalle, being easily the senior among the priests present, who would often preside. Father Willigis Jäeger, OSB, a Benedictine monk who himself became a renowned Zen Master in Europe, who had stayed in

Kamakura receiving Yamada Roshi's guidance for a number of years in the seventies and eighties, would also occasionally be the presiding priest at these Eucharistic celebrations held during sesshin.

From the late seventies through the eighties, given renewed confidence by his own Zen teacher's approval, Father Lassalle spent a few months of the year in Europe guiding Zen retreats, wherein the Eucharist would always be a daily feature. Here is an account by a participant of German nationality (who is now my beloved spouse) at one of those retreats, providing an insider's view of Father Lassalle's way of guiding Christian practitioners on the Zen path.

ॐ

Providence led me to Father Lassalle in the spring of 1982, at a crucial moment for my spiritual path in life. In fall of 1981, I had enrolled in Chinese and Japanese studies at the Ludwig Maximilians University in Munich after a two-year stay in Taiwan where I had immersed myself in Chinese language and culture. Having been raised Catholic, I encountered Buddhism for the first time in Taiwan. When I shared my good intentions to write a Master's thesis on Chinese Buddhism with my Buddhist teacher in Taiwan, Master Hsin Tao—now well known as the founder of the Museum of World Religions in Taipei—he advised me that, unless I started a regular meditation practice, I would not know what I was writing about. Taking this seriously, I was looking and asking around for a Zen teacher in Munich. As luck would have it, a friend offered me his place in a retreat to be led by Father Lassalle, whom I had not heard about before. As there were always long waiting lists for Father Lassalle's retreats, I sent him a letter, explaining my situation and asking for permission to take my friend's place. To my surprise, I very soon received a positive, hand-written response from Father Lassalle himself. With all of the retreats he was leading in Europe at that time, in addition to those in Japan, he still found the time to answer me.

The retreat was held at the Franciscan monastery in Diet-furt, a beautiful place with a traditional, Japanese style Zendo with a lush garden outside. This was my very first six-day Zen retreat ever, and I was full of questions. The most basic question I posed to Father Lassalle on the first day was this: "Wouldn't Jesus mind if I started practicing Buddhist medi-tation?" Father Lassalle, dressed in his black priestly outfit, looked at me with a reassuring, slightly amused smile and said after a brief pause, "You know what—I wouldn't worry about this." I took this on his Jesuit authority and stopped worrying. But when I came back the next day to ask if it would be okay for me to enter a Buddhist monastery in Taiwan—an option I had been contemplating—he didn't smile. "Aren't you Chris-tian?" he asked me with a searching look. "Don't imagine that you will find enlightenment simply by moving into a Buddhist monastery. You have to practice right where you are. Also, you cannot awaken if you have any preferences in your mind. Keep your mind open, without any judgments."

Meditationshaus St. Franziskus in Dietfurt, Germany, the first Zendo in a Christian monastery.

Father Lassalle was very charismatic as a teacher. He gently and deeply drew us into the presence of the Divine—just by sitting in silence with us in the Zendo, sometimes dozing off on the cushion, taking a meal, giving the same talks on the three fruits of Zen and the new consciousness from his torn old notebook, or taking us on with his knowing and yet humorous gaze during Dokusan. His celebration of daily Mass in a small tatami chapel was for me the most powerful experience in all of this. We would sit in a circle in deep silence, with hardly any words spoken except for one reading and the words of the consecration. When Father Lassalle lifted up the bread and wine in complete silence, the mystery and grace at the heart of our existence became as palpable for me as never before. My boundless joy and gratitude at the end of each retreat was also a new experience for me.

After one or two more retreats, Father Lassalle found me ready to work with the koan Mu—which is given to all beginners in the Sanbo Zen tradition. Working with this koan for six years led me to one light-filled moment in which all barriers keeping me from perceiving each and every one of us and the whole universe filled by grace and love just fell away. When I went to see Father Lassalle in Dokusan and gave him the answer to my koan, which I had realized through the experience, he seemed a bit surprised and said—"Yes, that's right. How did this come to you?" And looking around for his notebook, he said "Let's see now, there are some checking questions we need to go through." Nothing special, no big deal, stay grounded and keep the practice going.

With boundless gratitude, Maria Reis

❧

Toward the late 1980s, also at a gathering over tea and cookies after a Zen retreat, Yamada Roshi addressed the group, noting the presence of Jewish and Christian participants of that sesshin. He was now nearing the age of eighty at the time, and there were a number who were in near completion of the koan curriculum offered at San-Un Zendo, having practiced already for many years under his guiding hand, koan after koan. (A number of those in that group were later designated as his Dharma heirs after Yamada Koun Roshi´s passing in September of 1989.) He told the group, "*As you all now know, the world of Zen that you came here to learn and experience cannot be captured by any words or concepts. My wish for you is that you continue to soak yourself into this world that is beyond any words or concepts, and experience it more and more deeply and thoroughly, that you may live in its light every day of your lives. Now, as you go back to your own countries, in order to impart this world of Zen to the people you meet there, you must take efforts to learn the religious concepts and expressions that those in your communities are familiar with, but without getting attached to them. Those of you who are Christians, read and learn about your Bible, Christian theology and so on, so that you may find suitable expressions there which you may use as the gateway in leading people to an experience of that world beyond words. I myself am Buddhist, so I have taught you using the Buddhist language and framework I am most familiar with. If you are Christian, you may take the words and concepts of your tradition to guide people in the world of Zen.*"

Hearing these words for me at the time was like receiving a mandate, a nudge forward on a path I felt moved to pursue during those years of practicing Zen under Yamada Roshi's guidance and beyond. It is a path that I continue to tread and explore to this day. Father Hugo Enomiya-Lassalle, S.J., had forged this path ahead of anyone else, and to him we all remain in profound debt and acknowledge undying gratitude.

—Ruben L. F. Habito, with Maria Reis Habito

Glossary

Absorption: a meditative state in which all subject-object related thinking ceases, yet a profound mental clarity prevails.

Acharya: spiritual teacher (Hindu traditions).

Ashram: center for religious studies and monastery (Hindu traditions).

Butsudan: altar with a Buddha statue and often statues of Bodhisattvas in the center of the zendo.

Contemplation: a Christian spiritual practice, which is described, for example, by St. John of the Cross as a way into the "dark night of the senses," the "dark night of the soul," and the "dark night of the mind"—a way of purification and absorption to be receptive to God's love, sometimes referred to as objectless meditation.

Buddha Mind/Buddha Nature: In Mahayana, the true, unchanging nature of all beings, interpreted differently by different schools. Also referred to as "absolute" or "absolute truth" in contrast to "conventional truth."

Darshan: experiencing blessing and purification through the sight of a saint, guru, or holy place (Hindu traditions).

Dharma: the teachings of Buddha, but also the cosmic law, and the moral law.

Discursive prayer: a method of Christian prayer in which the contents of the Holy Scriptures are recollected (Christianity). In medieval times this was called "meditation."

Dokusan: literally "going alone," a private encounter between a Zen master and a disciple.

Eucharist: literally "thanksgiving," or "Mass," a celebration to remember Jesus Christ´s life, death, and resurrection.

Gojukai: the five moral obligations of Buddhist lay people (see *sila*).

Jesus Prayer or Prayer of the Heart: A Christian meditation tradition practiced mainly in Orthodox churches, but today also more and more by Catholics and other denominations. The formula "Lord Jesus Christ, have mercy on me" (or a shorter version) is repeated with each inhalation and exhalation.

Jikijitsu: the monk in charge of the zendo.

Jiriki: "self-power," in contrast to "other power." In Zen, it is sometimes said that one can achieve satori through one's own efforts.

Joriki: "power of concentration." This refers to a meditator's ability to enter into and maintain a deep meditative state even outside of formal practice.

Kensho: literally "looking at your own true nature," in Zen the first experience of awakening.

Koan: literally "public case," very often sayings or short stories about Zen masters and students in the "golden age of Zen," given as a means of training to the students. It is a paradox that can only be solved by shifting to a level of understanding that surpasses the rational.

Kyosaku: literally "awakening stick," used in the Zendo to encourage meditators. A well-placed tap on the shoulders stimulates acupuncture points.

Makyo: The characteristic psychophysiological phenomena that indicate that body and mind are gradually beginning to calm down. Any mental state which is not liberation, satori.

Meditation: meditation often refers not to a specific method, but rather to a general attitude toward spiritual practice of any kind. See also "discursive prayer."

Mu: "no," "nothing." In contexts of Zen it refers to the Koan "Joshu and the Dog." Mumonkan Case 1.

Muga: "no-self," refers to the basic teaching of Buddhism, that there is no permanent "self."

Ofuro: a hot bath, Japanese style. First you have to clean yourself, then you sit in a shared basin filled with very hot water.

Prasad: literally "God's grace and benevolence"; sacrificial food offered to the deity and then returned to the faithful, said to contain spiritual powers (Hindu traditions).

Rinzai-shu: one of the two major schools of Zen Buddhism, emphasizes practice with koans.

Sanbokyodan: "Order of the Three Treasures," an independent religious group founded by Yasutani Roshi. Recently the group changed the name to "Sanbo Zen."

Sanzenkai: an association of Zen practitioners.

Satori: literally "comprehension," but without an object; in Zen the full experience of awakening.

Sesshins: full days devoted to sitting on a cushion, face to the wall, meditating in complete silence.

Sila: commitments or commandments in Buddhism. There are five fundamental commitments: refraining from killing, not taking what is not given, avoiding illicit sexual relations, abstaining from unwholesome speech, and refraining from intoxicants.

Soto-shu: one of the two major schools of Zen Buddhism, emphasizes the practice of shikantaza, or "just sitting."

Storehouse Consciousness: a central concept of the Yogacara school of Mahayana Buddhism. A fundamental aspect of reality, contains the "seeds" of all phenomena of all times.

Tabor-Light or Uncreated Light: the peak experience in the practice of the Prayer of the Heart in Eastern Orthodox Christianity. Refers to the transfiguration of Christ on Mount Tabor (Mt 17:8–1; Mk 9:2–13; Lk 9:28–36).

Tariki: "other power" in contrast to jiriki (see there). In the Pure Land Schools of Buddhism, they say that one is liberated through trust in the salvific power of Amida Buddha.

Teisho: formal talk given by a Zen teacher that shares her/his direct, experiential understanding of the Dharma. Very often a teisho is about a koan, or a classical Zen text.

Tenno: "Heavenly Emperor"; title of the Japanese emperor.

Theravada: literally "School of the Elders," Buddhism in Southeast Asia based exclusively on the Pali Canon.

Zaibatsu: financially powerful conglomerates owned by a clan or family.

Zazen: literally "sitting in absorption."

Zendo: the meditation hall in a Zen temple; any room for formal Zen practice, sometimes also a community practicing together.

॰

Note: Diacritical marks have been ommitted to make the text easier to read.

Books by
H. M. Enomiya-Lassalle

Hiroshima (Spanish), Buenos Aires, 1948 (reprint 2015; trans. German)

Shinri to Onkei, Tokyo, 1959/1969.

Zen-Weg zur Erleuchtung, Wien/Freiburg 1960, (trans. Spanish, French, Japanese, Korean, Dutch, English)

Zen-Buddhismus, Köln 1966.

Zen-Meditation für Christen, Weilheim 1973 (trans. Dutch, Spanish, French, Japanese, Swedish).

Meditation als Weg zur Gotteserfahrung, Köln 1973 (trans. Dutch, Japanese).

Zen-Meditation – eine Einführung, Zürich/Einsiedeln/Köln 1975 (new title: Kraft aus dem Schweigen).

Zazen und die Exerzitien des heiligen, Ignatius, Köln 1975.

Zen-Meditation. Eine Einführung, Einsiedeln 1972.

Zen und christliche Mystik, Freiburg 1986, (rev. edition of *Zen-Buddhismus,*1966)

Zen und christliche Spiritualität, München 1986.

Wohin geht der Mensch?, Zürich 1981; new title: *Am Morgen einer besseren Welt: Der Mensch im Durchbruch zu einem neuen Bewusstsein* (Herderbucherei, 1984).

English Translations:

Zen: Way to Enlightenment (1964).

Zen Meditation for Christians (1974).

Living the New Consciousness (1984).

The Practice of Zen Meditation (1987).

Index